foreword by JAMES W. GOLL

WHEN

stories of

GENERATIONS

elijahs

RUN

and elishas

TOGETHER

Patricia King • Bill Hamon • Che Ahn • Jane Hamon
Ryan LeStrange • Barbara Yoder • Joshua Giles
Sherman Dumas • Tony Kim • Jamie Galloway

compiled by ELIZABETH TIAM-FOOK

Marcy—
Thank you for loving the generations.

ISBN: 978-0-578-37653-0

internationalyoungprophets.com

For worldwide distribution

WHEN GENERATIONS RUN TOGETHER

Stories of Elijahs and Elishas

Elijah said to Elisha, "Ask me what I should do for you before I am taken from you." And Elisha said, "Please let a double portion of your spirit be upon me." He said, "You have asked a hard thing. Nevertheless, if you see me when I am taken from you, it shall be so for you; but if not, it shall not be so."

2 Kings 1:9,10

ENDORSEMENTS

When Generations Run Together is a much needed resource for those wanting their life to be bigger than themselves. The chapters are written by people who have done the hard thing of turning their hearts to spiritual sons and daughters or to spiritual fathers and mothers. We know them personally. They have lived the life of an Elijah and/or Elisha. We want to do that too. This book is full of practical helps. Thank you, Elizabeth, for bringing this wisdom to print for us all.

JIM AND BECKY HENNESY
TRINITY CHURCH
CEDAR HILL, TEXAS

Elizabeth has successfully unveiled the power of generations in *When Generations Run Together*. God specializes in generational success, and now the church must take the torch and ignite the generations coming behind us! This book is a must read for anyone wanting to live a life of impact and legacy.

MARK AND PATRICIA ESTES
NORTH PALM GLOBAL
CHARLESTON, SOUTH CAROLINA

What an amazing book! *When Generations Run Together* will transform your heart and life. We all want a spiritual father or mother who will champion us on and encourage our destiny. And it's equally important to know how to be a good son or daughter. The wisdom found in these pages from authentic spiritual leaders will not only teach you how to be a leader but also a father or mother. The younger generation desperately needs this. You will also learn how to walk in humility and honor in a way that will unleash God's blessing on your life—a double portion mantle. This book needs to be read by every spiritual leader and by those who desire to lead. Elizabeth's testimony is inspiring, as well as each leader's personal journey and experience found in this book. It deeply impacted me. I know it will impact you!

MATT SORGER
MATT SORGER MINISTRIES
WAXHAW, NORTH CAROLINA

Elizabeth Tiam-Fook is a new breed of prophet with a heart for seeing the merging of generations and the company of prophets rise up with the spirit and power of Elijah. This book exemplifies her heart and mission by combining the wisdom of seasoned "Elijahs" and revelation from seasoned "Elishas" to help pave the way for revival and reformation. I highly recommend this book to any believer hungry to grow in their walk with God.

IVAN ROMAN
EMPOWERED LIFE CHURCH
MEDFORD, OREGON

Joining the generations is one of the primary messages on God's heart in this season. Revival and reformation cannot be sustained or advanced by merely one generational demographic but rather must be synergized by a multi-generational effort. God's grace is multiplied and the next generation arises with a renewed vision and bold demonstration when the power of impartation is released from one generation to the next. Only then will we see a healthy and powerful church arise with an ability to see God's Kingdom come and transform culture, cities, and nations.

TOM HAMON
VISION CHURCH AT CHRISTIAN INTERNATIONAL
SANTA ROSA BEACH, FLORIDA

A popular cultural phrase states, "Knowledge is only a rumor until it lives in the muscle." We learn many lessons in the classroom, but most of the "fruit that remains" in our lives is forged in the fires of everyday living. Elizabeth's gift for gathering mature prophetic leaders to help mentor budding next-gen prophets places her in an Esther 4:14 moment: she is here for "such a time as this." This book provides many rich summary samples of lessons learned, from both the early prophetic pioneers and the emerging prophetic leaders who will carry these mantles forward.

Elizabeth has earned her prophetic muscle-memory the old-fashioned way: by serving under these generals of the faith. This book follows the rapid-fire format Elizabeth developed with the "We Prophesy" events she hosts around the country. We glean the wisdom of ten different prophets, each writing a chapter that captures essential foundational aspects of their ministries.

Prophets are courageous people, waking up every day with a willingness to yield to the authority and guidance of God's Spirit living in them. We would do well to "consider our ways" (Haggai 1:7) and follow the priceless advice these visionary leaders provide in the book you are holding in your hands.

PETER AND TRISHA ROSELLE
KING OF KINGS WORSHIP CENTER
BASKING RIDGE, NEW JERSEY

Each generation is entrusted with the joy and responsibility of stewarding what has been given to them from those who have preceded us. Within the story of Elijah and Elisha, we see a beautiful picture of what multigenerational living, honor, and spiritual inheritance should look like. Within the pages of this book, Elizabeth has artfully woven together a tapestry of principles, sound wisdom, and faith-filled stories from proven leaders, all who share from their own unique journey. These stories provide a roadmap that any lover of Jesus can learn from. We wholeheartedly endorse this book and pray it brings clarity, freedom, and connection to all who read it. We love you, Elizabeth, and thank you for providing such a timely resource to encourage and strengthen Kingdom relationships for generations to come.

JIM AND RENEE CUTTER
REGENCY CHURCH
WHITTIER, CALIFORNIA

DEDICATION

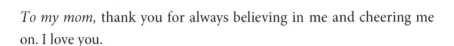

To my mom, thank you for always believing in me and cheering me on. I love you.

To Bishop Bill Hamon, you have been a source of strength and direction, plus a wonderful spiritual father, and our dream to see God's Company of Prophets "run together" will be seen in the days ahead.

To Ché Ahn, one of the reasons this book has been written is because of you. Thank you for challenging me to believe for our nation to be transformed and for modeling the apostolic and fatherhood to my generation.

To Patricia King, my pastor, thank you for always breathing life into my dreams and heart. You have ALWAYS believed in me. Thank you for living a life in a way that a whole generation can follow after.

To Jane Hamon, my Elijah, from the time I saw you when I was a teenager to now, you have lived a life that makes me believe that we can see cities and regions transform.

To all the Elishas, keep running with and loving your Elijahs well. Your inheritance and double portion are worth it.

To all the Elijahs, a whole generation needs your love, time, strength, hope, and patience. Thank you for being willing to pay the price for legacy and see God's Kingdom advance.

To International Young Prophets, thank you for the joy of serving you all. The prophetic movement is so blessed to have your voices raised up for this hour. What a privilege we all get to "run together" to serve His Church and the nations.

TABLE OF CONTENTS

FOREWORD

James W. Goll

President/Founder
God Encounters Ministries
Franklin, Tennessee

In the Book of Genesis, God identifies Himself as the God of three generations in one generation: the God of Abraham, Isaac, and Jacob. I believe there is precedent to state, that when there is a sustained move of the Holy Spirit, God manifests Himself as the God of three generations in a generation. In the Book of Joel, when referencing the global outpouring of the Holy Spirit, we find, "Your old men shall dream dreams, your young men shall see visions." It takes a young man's vision to fulfill an old man's dream—again, a reference to the synergy of the generations.

In fact, this theme of the joining of the generations is found throughout the Scriptures. I have often stated that it takes the wisdom of the older, the resources of the middle, and the zeal of the younger generation working in tandem together to be fruitful in the long term.

Years ago, I had a pivotal and invitational God Encounter. I was alone, seeking the Lord with prayer and fasting while I was staying at a cabin. Late at night, I felt the leading of the Holy Spirit to go on a walk. Jesus drew ever so near as one friend to another. His voice came to me, speaking words of wisdom: "You have a choice to make. You can build a raft for you and your family, or you can build many sailboats and send them forth to the nations. The choice is yours to make."

That exchange marked my life. I made an overt decision, that my goal was not about how big of a ministry platform I would have for myself, but rather, one of my priorities would be helping others achieve their dreams. Yes, it has been one of my personal goals for years, no matter what size of a platform I have, to share it with others. I love investing in others. Mentoring takes time, but it is an investment that will ultimately pay off.

So whether it's Elijah and Elisha, Moses and Joshua, Samuel and the School of the Prophets, Jesus and His twelve, or Paul and Timothy, it's a key to multiplication. After all, it's the model and lifestyle of Jesus.

With gratefulness,
James W. Goll

INTRODUCTION

Elizabeth Tiam Fook

Founder
International Young Prophets
Maricopa, Arizona

While attending a conference in Orlando about eight years ago, I didn't know that my life would be marked that day by a scripture that would unfold in my life within the next couple of years. I was in a break-out session, and the speaker was Ché Ahn, an apostle and pastor in California. He opened up his session by saying that God sometimes used him through a scripture that impacted people's lives. That afternoon he shared Malachi 4:5-6. These two verses impacted me so much that I didn't hear anything else he said after that. I knew the message that afternoon was for me, and I knew God was speaking to me.

As time went on, the Lord invited me on a personal journey where He began to speak to me about Elijah and Elisha. I recognized that I, too, was an Elisha. Since then, I've sat down and talked with a number of other "Elishas" over the years. Surely, we are all thankful for the mentorship and impartation we receive from our Elijahs. At the same time, all have agreed with the following: "It's hard."

The prophet Elisha modeled this for us when Elijah was about to be taken away. Elijah asked Elisha what he could do for him. After Elisha told him he wanted a double portion of his spirit, Elijah answered, "You have asked a difficult thing….yet if you see me when I am taken from you, it will be yours—otherwise, it will not."

It's so sad when there is an expectation that a mantle will be passed on to a certain person, but for some reason it ends up not happening. But watching it pass on to someone and then witnessing that person become transformed by the "assignment of the mantle"…that's beautiful to see. That's the goal of this book.

The more I studied this scripture and witnessed both possible outcomes in ministry, business, and other scenarios, I realized that I had never heard a teaching on the warfare involved on the way to receiving the double portion.

I have wonderful Elijahs that God has brought into my life, and as an Elisha who is desiring to grow and mature in my calling, I can say that God has allowed opportunities through interactions with my Elijahs to test my character and calling. I always long to honor and respect them even when there is a misunderstanding. As a result, I've painfully discovered the value of humbling myself and listening carefully and prayerfully rather than being self-protective and defensive. You quickly learn that it is better to "do what is right" rather than "be right."

There have been times during a confrontation or misunderstanding that I've felt totally crushed. These tests weren't necessarily about the Elijah, even if at the time, it seemed to me that they were the one in the wrong. God was testing me to see if I believed in the calling and was willing to humble myself and let Christ be formed in me... and still be standing by my Elijah at the end of the day. He was looking to see if I would trust Him and trust the process He was taking me through to receive the double portion.

Just as Elijah told Elisha, "It's difficult....yet if you see me, you will receive what you requested." There is something about still standing next to your Elijah after the difficult moments. But if you are still standing, you WILL receive the double portion.

If you are an Elijah, know that to see the fruit of the legacy that you are imparting to the next generation, the hard times will be worth it in the end. Remember that the higher the call, the tougher the process. Be willing to stand by your Elisha and fight the war to see both of you win. Ultimately, the Kingdom of God wins when generations run together.

We as the Church are in a prophetic season in which we will see Malachi 4:5-6 and 2 Kings 2 manifest in front of our eyes. The hearts of the fathers are turning to the children.

I pray that as you read this book, it will help and encourage you on your journey, whether you are an Elijah or an Elisha. I pray that if you have been hurt, you will allow God into your heart to help and heal you to continue the process.

Elijah's LEGACY is in Elisha and Elisha's DESTINY is in Elijah. When generations are willing to pay the price and run together, we will see families become whole, cities transformed, and nations saved.

Elijah's LEGACY is in Elisha and Elisha's DESTINY is in Elijah. When generations are willing to pay the price and run together, we will see families become whole, cities transformed, and nations saved.

Chapter One

ATTRIBUTES OF SPIRITUAL FATHERS AND MOTHERS

Patricia King

Founder
Patricia King Ministries
Maricopa, Arizona

When I came to the Lord in my early twenties, I did not have any specific individual to disciple or mentor me in my faith or calling. My first pastor was facing his own struggles with a congregation that did not want to move forward with him in the charismatic renewal. He graciously released me to pursue my passion to know Holy Spirit and encouraged me to connect with a Spirit-filled church. My next pastor was mostly focused on building his church and vision. However, he fed us great insights from the Word on Sunday mornings, and the presence of the Lord was truly evident. Every Sunday there were numerous salvations, and many others were baptized in the Spirit. He brought in Spirit-filled evangelists and teachers who empowered us as well, and I was blessed with many peer friendships who were also extremely passionate for God. They were all amazing gifts, and their input helped me grow!

In my third year of coming to Jesus, I had the privilege of sitting under the teaching of Mary Goddard—a very anointed woman of God who has now passed on to glory—for a five-month course on the gifts of the Spirit. Right after that, my husband and I, along with our two children, headed to YWAM Kona (Hawaii) for a six-month program in discipleship, where we received great teaching. Then we labored as part of a YWAM leadership team in Belize for six months. Following our return, Mary Goddard took my husband and me with her to Africa on a ministry trip and opened doors for me to share the gospel. Later, I was invited to join her ministry as the Evangelism Director.

All these people, experiences, and opportunities were true blessings. The Holy Spirit also used many people to parent and disciple me along the way through books, audio and videotapes, and other resources. But as I look back, I cannot identify any individual I would call my spiritual father or mother, and I honestly have never felt that one was missing in my life. In fact, back in the day, you didn't hear much about spiritual fathers and mothers.

If you are reading this book and think that you are experiencing a deficit because you can't identify a committed spiritual parent in your life, I want to encourage you. The Holy Spirit has been extravagantly given to us by our Heavenly Father to teach, guide, and mentor us. He is with you and will give you everything you need, and He will be all things to you.

David said in Psalm 27:10, "When my father and my mother forsake me, then the Lord will take me up" (KJV). He truly understood this through what he had experienced in his life. I too was wonderfully parented because the Lord took me up! God will do the same for you.

Having stated that encouragement, we can't ignore the strong prophetic voice of the Lord in this day in calling for His divine model to emerge: the hearts of the fathers (parents) turning to the children and the children to the fathers (parents).

> Behold, I will send you Elijah the prophet before the coming of the great and dreadful day of the Lord: And he shall turn the heart of the fathers to the children, and the heart of the children to their fathers, lest I come and smite the earth with a curse. (Malachi 4:5,6 KJV)

For the sake of definition, I refer to "fathers" as spiritual mothers and fathers and "children" as the next generation(s) of believers and leaders.

I personally have never asked anyone if I could be their spiritual mother, but I have many who call me this. Every time I hear someone call me a spiritual mom I am humbled, and my spirit is once again awakened with the responsibility of such a call and privilege to serve. I have been on a journey the last number of years, exploring the responsibilities of mothering spiritually and the grace that is available. It is not something to be taken lightly, but rather with reverence and sobriety.

We are called as spiritual parents to model godly values and character for the next generation(s) in a general sense, but God is also

We are called as spiritual parents to model godly values and character for the next generation(s) in a general sense, but God is also calling those who are mature in Him to parent and nurture specific individuals that His grace *appoints.*

calling those who are mature in Him to parent and nurture specific individuals that His grace appoints. According to Malachi 4:5,6, it is vital for us as fathers and mothers in the faith to turn our hearts to the next generation in order for all to continue to live in blessing rather than curse.

When Elizabeth Tiam-Fook asked me to contribute a chapter to this book, I struggled to pin-point a specific focus to write on, as this is a massive topic that requires so much insight. I finally settled on unpacking what I have learned to be the three most important attributes of a spiritual parent. I will share more from a maternal perspective, but I believe the following attributes are characteristics our Father in Heaven is looking for in the lives of those who parent the coming generation(s). Malachi describes the order: parents turn to the children first, and then the children turn to the parents.

THREE IMPORTANT GODLY ATTRIBUTES OF SPIRITUAL PARENTS

1. The Attribute of Godliness

About a year ago, I was conversing with a young man who was sharing his journey into ministry. He revealed that his mentor and spiritual covering in his ministry had been exposed publicly as a drunkard, womanizer, sex addict, abuser, and deceiver, as well as a poor steward of ministry finances. His heart was broken, and he felt deeply betrayed, not only concerning the ungodly actions of his "spiritual father" but also due to this individual's lack of repentance and ownership of the multiple confirmed allegations. This young man was crushed, not knowing how to move forward. His mentor and overseer was very anointed and had a winning, charismatic personality. How could he manifest so much of God's presence, yet live in so much darkness?

This young man admitted that he had witnessed behaviors in his mentor's life that crossed moral lines, but at the time, he shrugged it off as something that simply needed to be covered by love and grace since he was so anointed.

As the founder of Voice4Victims—a ministry that gives support to those who have been abused sexually, emotionally, spiritually, or financially in the church—I hear too many stories like this young man's.

Paul, on the other hand, encourages believers to follow him as he follows the Lord:

> "Follow my example, as I follow the example of Christ." (1 Corinthians 11:1 NIV)

Paul had confidence that if believers followed him as he followed the Lord, they would not stumble. Are you living a godly life? Are people safe to follow you? I always encourage my team and those I serve as a spiritual mother to live their lives in such a way that if children were to do what we do and say what we say, they would not stumble in life but rather have solid truth and values established in their lives.

> But whoever causes one of these little ones who believe in Me to sin, it is better for him that a heavy millstone be hung around his neck, and that he be drowned in the depths of the sea. (Matthew 18:6)

If you are going to be a spiritual father or mother to the next generation(s), you cannot live carelessly, giving in to fleshly indulgences or to the love of the world and its lusts. As spiritual parents, we must partake of the divine nature and model it well without double standards. Raise the bar high.

A well-respected man of God who will be remembered throughout mankind's history and into eternity is the late Reverend Billy Graham. As a successful evangelist, millions upon millions came to the Lord through his ministry. However, he is not only honored for the fruit of his ministry but also for his godly character. Even the unsaved masses favored Billy Graham. He was a man whom people trusted and regarded, and he became a beloved spiritual father on a global level. Not only did he bring many into the Kingdom, but he discipled many through his teachings and his example of godliness.

The church and the world desperately need godly examples today. In society, we see rebellion, dishonor, lawlessness, immorality, faithlessness, and offense. What if in this current generation we see the emergence of radical believers who are obedient, honoring, lawful, moral, faith-empowered, and unoffendable because they have had spiritual parents model and teach these Kingdom values? I long for this. Let's make it happen!

What if in this current generation we see the emergence of radical believers who are obedient, honoring, lawful, moral, faith-empowered, and unoffendable because they have had spiritual parents model and teach these Kingdom values?

---

2. The Attribute of Selfless Love and Care

Motives of the heart are everything! Love always desires the highest good for the sake of another and is not motivated by selfish gain. The spiritual fathers and mothers God is raising up in this hour are those who embrace the cross—death to selfish ambition and motives. They give themselves to the next generation because they love them!

It is very easy to say, "I love you," but it is often challenging to walk it out. Your love will be tested over and over again. In a natural family, you will at times find one of the children to be more challenging than the others. They try your patience, and sometimes you might wonder if they will turn out well. Yet, in watching these dynamics in families over the years, I've observed that often, the most trying children are the ones who accomplishes the most in their adult years. It's interesting to watch. Likewise, as a spiritual parent, you will at times need "love eyes" in order to see beyond the "stone in the rough."

Some of my most fruitful, successful, and beloved children in the faith required me to see them through God's love potential in their early journeys. In fact, some of them had so many visible rough edges that I often had other believers and friends warn me about my involvement with them because they "discerned" their challenging issues. God will help you see way beyond those things… and you will need to if you are going to love well.

All things are possible with God. I often see my spiritual children like flowers in bud form with all their potential beauty within. I remember a rose bush that was given to us as a gift years ago. It was a thorny group of brown stems in a pot of dirt when we received it from a friend. It didn't look like much, but we proceeded reluctantly to plant it in the garden.

Although it appeared to be without promise initially, it had hidden potential that would eventually amaze us. The bush grew tender leaves, and then small, closed buds came into visibility. The plant continued to grow over time, and the buds emerged with a glory of their own. As they opened fully, they offered a great surprise. I will never forget the first rose that fully opened. It boasted multiple colors, with shades of light coral, yellow, pink, and orange. It smelled like sweet peaches and was massive in size—about the size of a large grapefruit. Then one bloom after another after another, we saw the entire bush come alive with beauty. Every year following, that rose bush produced the most beautiful flowers. Many were elated when they gazed upon that bush and its blooms and smelled its fragrance. What began as a pot of dirt, sticks, and thorns was transformed into something of great value that blessed many. All that beauty was hidden in the original pot. I never would have guessed at first glance what the full potential was.

There is so much potential in each precious life God brings to us, and as spiritual fathers and mothers, we have the opportunity to both see and nurture that potential. I believe Jesus modeled this when He chose His twelve disciples. They were all pretty rough and unpolished, but those twelve transformed the world. Jesus saw their potential.

Another aspect of love is caring for your spiritual children when they experience hurts and disappointments. Life is full of painful moments and circumstances, and sometimes your spiritual children will need a generous dose of reassurance …and a big hug! As a spiritual parent, you are not required to "fix" the problem unless it is wise to do so and you are able, but rather to help your spiritual children know how to lean on the Lord as they walk through their dark and disappointing moments. When you are there alongside them, it gives them strength. You might need to give up some time, sleep, and comfort of your own, but that is what selfless love looks like.

When you choose to love, you will bond with your spiritual children and will know how to give care and nurture to them in their time of need. We always want to encourage them to be bold, confident, courageous and not co-dependent, but there are times when they will need extra reassurance.

Like natural parenting, spiritual parenting is an honor and a privilege, but it also requires sacrifice. You would never use your spiritual children to give yourself advantage; rather, like Jesus, you lay your life down for them, serving them well. When you love them beautifully and fully, they will one day rise up and bless you because of the seed you have selflessly sown into them.

There is so much potential in each precious life God brings to us, and as spiritual fathers and mothers, we have the opportunity to both see and nurture that potential. Jesus modeled this ... His twelve disciples were all pretty rough and unpolished, but they transformed the world. Jesus saw their potential!

3. The Attribute of Generosity

There are so many things to extravagantly and intentionally sow into your spiritual children and the next generation. You have probably heard the phrase, "Our ceiling is the next generation's floor."

This is regarding the building of a legacy. What do you possess that can be sown into the next generation?

Recently, I have been enjoying reflections of all the Lord has taught me over the 45-plus years I have known Him. I've come to realize that there were many things that I took for granted. A nugget of wisdom or a truth revealed can easily become so normalized in your own life that you fail to realize there are many who have never been introduced to those things. I've been intentionally preparing teachings and mentorship groups in order to share some of these nuggets, insights, and revelations. I want to intentionally and generously sow into the next generation what the Lord has so richly granted me.

Another area the Lord has been speaking to me about is to generously sow my time. Many times in a day I will be on the phone or engage in texting with those I love and nurture or spend time in prayers and decrees for them. Engagement with one another builds bonds, but it takes time and availability.

I also have been investing my time into the dreams and assignments of my spiritual children and often running alongside of them as they forge their trails. When you do this, you build memories, and this is so important and enriching. Jesus modeled doing life with His disciples. They ministered, ate, and travelled together. As He gave them His time, they bonded, and much of the rich and profound input and impartation He poured into the disciples' lives was "as they went."

We always desire our spiritual children to cultivate their own precious journey with the Lord and to utilize their faith to fulfill God's purposes, but we must also be sensitive to what they need from us along the way. It is an honor to give and to bless.

As parents of natural children, we provide for their needs such as food, clothing, and shelter, but we teach them as they grow to exercise their own abilities to produce from their own initiative. We must train them to stir their ability to prosper and see dreams and goals fulfilled.

I remember my oldest son at age 11 sharing how much he wanted a computer when they first came on the market decades ago. My husband and I did not have the means to purchase it for him at the time, but I said, "You can surely have your dream come true. You can work at your paper route, save your money, and buy one. God will help you, and we will be in your cheering section!" We generously shared wisdom with him on how to define his dream, set goals, work hard, and steward what came into his hand. This was what we had in our hand to give at the time.

We contributed financially what we could from time to time, but for the most part, he raised all the money on his own. He worked hard to make the money to purchase the computer. He saved every penny and sacrificed other things in order to see his dream come true. After a number of months, he was able to purchase it. If we had bought the computer for him, he never would have experienced the faith journey he walked, the lessons he learned, or the fulfillment he felt. Over the years, the Lord blessed him greatly. Today, he is in his late forties and is a hard worker and a good steward of resources. He has been blessed with great bounty.

As spiritual parents, it is an honor to sow resource and finances into our spiritual children as the Lord leads and in the right timing. We have joyfully sown much into the next generation, but we do so strategically and with wisdom so that they also flex their own faith muscles. It is a wonderful blessing to partner with the next generation of believers as they walk out their destiny.

Our Father in Heaven is an extravagant giver. He gave His own Son for all. There is no good or beneficial thing that He has withheld from us. This generous nature is in us as believers, and we are to generously bless our spiritual children with the riches He has given to us.

There are so many attributes that we could study and embrace, but I have found these three to be the greatest core values for serving the next generation as spiritual mothers or fathers.

May we be the generation that sees the hearts of the fathers restored to the children…and the children to the fathers. What a glorious way that will produce a glorious day!

Chapter Two

PROPHETIC MENTORING

Dr. Bill Hamon

Founder/Bishop
Christian International Apostolic Network
Santa Rosa Beach, Florida

There has been much discussion through the years concerning the mentoring process for developing ministers. One of the examples used from the Old Testament is that of Elijah and Elisha. Some use the terms spiritual fathers and mothers ministering to spiritual sons and daughters.

I have two natural sons. Tim, the oldest, attended secular colleges where he earned his Bachelor's and Master's degrees. He worked for Honeywell for years, and then in 1988, he moved to Florida to work with Christian International (CI). Tim is an Apostolic Teacher and ministers some in the prophetic.

Tom is my second son. I have had the opportunity to be an Elijah to him. He received the call of God to preach when he was 12 years old. He attended Life Bible College in Los Angeles and earned his Bachelor's, Master's, and Doctorate degrees. After graduation, he came to work full time with CI. He married Jane, and in1984, they joined us in Florida, where we had started prophetic training seminars. They also became pastors of the CI headquarters church in Santa Rosa Beach, Florida, in 1985, and have maintained that position for the last 36 years.

Tom also traveled with me in ministry at times. He often stood with me for hours, holding the mic while I did most of the prophesying. He was also called to be a prophet, and it was prophesied that he would have a double portion of his father's anointing. These are the reasons I use my son Tom to portray the Elijah-Elisha in mentoring or father-son relationship, both in the natural and the spiritual. My revelations on the Elijah-Elisha relationship are that God wants the older generation and the younger generation to run together until the older generation departs this world.

Another great example of a senior prophet raising up younger prophets is Samuel, through his Schools of Prophets. Samuel developed schools for training of the prophets, and he trained hundreds who looked to him as their father prophet. However, there is no indication that Samuel ever had one young prophet that he mentored and trained personally during the years of his ministry.

I have been a Samuel-type prophet to hundreds of prophets who have been trained in our Schools of the Prophets. We have established training centers in churches and in businesses around the world. I also wrote three prophetic books that have been used to educate, impart, activate, and train the younger generations.

A REPRODUCER OF REPRODUCERS

I received a prophecy in 1984 from an old prophet that God was giving me a ministry of reproducing reproducers who would become reproducers of reproducers. I started training about 15 young ministers who were mostly in their 20s. Three of them were Tom and Jane Hamon and Leon Walters. At first, I would have them stand with me while I prophesied, but then I would start to prophesy in the same manner I did when traveling alone. I would flow in prophecy three to five minutes, and then I would ask them if they had received anything to give. They would say, "Yes, but you already prophesied it."

The Lord then instructed me not to prophesy everything I saw, but to give only one or two points of what I was receiving to the person. When I did that and then let the others prophesy, they would cover all the other points plus even more than what I had seen and wanted to say to that individual.

In 1985, I came back from meetings in Australia not feeling well. We had a seminar scheduled that week. Usually, I would do all the preaching and prophesying for 36 hours of ministry during the three-day seminar. This time I told Tom and Jane that I was not going to be able to do all the teaching and prophesying over those present. I told them, "I am going to divide you up into teams of two and three each, and the teams will prophesy over all the attendees." It was a real challenge to them. They said, "These ministers did not come to receive from us but from you." I said, "No, they came to hear from God through the prophetic utterance." The teams did the prophesying, and all the attendees were satisfied and encouraged by the words they received. That is how we started having prophetic teams.

By 1989, we were forming 10-12 teams and prophesying over 400-500 attendees during our events. In 1993, we had close to 1,000 attendees. We formed 50 teams and assigned 20 attendees to each team. We prophesied to over 1,000 attendees in two hours. This came after several years of mentoring, fathering with teaching, impartation, activating, training, and maturing in prophetic ministry.

There is no record that Elisha did any prophesying or working of miracles while Elijah was still alive. I, on the other hand, activate those who run with me to prophesy right away and continue having them do more and more prophetic ministry until they are doing it as well as or better than I do. Tom and Jane, Apostle Leon Walters, Sharon Stone, and several hundred others have been mentored and fathered in the last 40 years. They prophesy as well as or better than I do now. I am fulfilling my prophetic commission to produce reproducers who reproduce others.

I have discovered that prophets and apostles seem to have more anointing and motivation for reproducing like kind. Too many pastors and teachers want to educate the mind by preaching and teaching rather than activating the spirit into manifesting the gifts of the Spirit. I have also noticed that some pastors know their people so well that they don't believe that they are mature enough to manifest the Spirit ministries. I must remind some of the ministers we have ordained in the ministry that they were not perfect and mature when we set them into their position and activated them into spiritual ministry. You can't learn to ride a bicycle just by hearing instruction. And you don't become a bicyclist just by sitting on the seat. You must take action and start peddling, learning to balance and ride the bicycle as you go peddling down the road. It's hard to get proficient in swimming if you never get in the water. In our training in the prophetic, we use Hebrews 5:14: "Those who by reason of use have their senses exercised to discern both good and evil." Our *Manual for Ministering Spiritual Gifts* is great, and it educates the mind, but the activations we have them do are what produce the experience needed to be proficient in prophesying.

Students and those being mentored must be given opportunity to exercise and practice what they have been taught or have seen manifest. As it says in James 2:22, "You must become doers of the word and not hearers only."

Students and those being mentored must be given opportunity to exercise and practice what they have been taught or have seen manifest. As it says in James 2:22, "You must become doers of the word and not hearers only."

MY STORY

My background is like Elijah's. We have no record of Elijah being mentored by an older prophet, and he didn't come from a priestly lineage. In like manner, I had no Christian background; there were no preachers in my past lineage—at least none that I know of. Also, I never had anyone to mentor me in ministry. I started pastoring when I was 19 years old. The church I pastored was an independent church and was not connected to any denomination or network of ministers and churches. I had no one to tutor me in being a pastor, and I had no one to tutor me in being a prophet. I guess because God called me to be a pioneer of moves of God, I had to do like the saying on Star Trek: "Go where no man has gone before."

I got exposed to prophetic presbytery in Bible college. Then, when I started pastoring, I attended the prophetic camp meetings for the next six years that were conducted by Pastor Reg Layzell, Pastor of Glade Tidings Temple in BC, Canada. He was the recognized Apostle of the Latter Rain Movement churches on the West Coast.

At the Bible college I attended in Portland, Oregon, three of the teachers announced they were going to conduct a laying on of hands and personal prophecy, which they called "prophetic presbytery." We students were told that in order to become a candidate to receive prophetic presbytery, we had to fast for three days and only have water. I was already on a six-day fast of water only, so I just continued my fast for three more days until the planned time on a Thursday night, October 1, 1953. Eighty of the students fasted to become candidates for prophetic presbytery. All of us sat on the first and second rows of the church, in hopes of being chosen to receive personal prophecy. Four teachers made up the prophetic presbytery. After an hour of worship, they joined together in a football-type huddle to pray and determine whom the Lord wanted to choose. They pointed to a brother who had been a missionary to Mexico for years. He appeared to be in his 40s, while most of the students ranged between 17-30. We wondered why they were calling up that "old man."

They had him kneel at a chair and laid hands on him while three of the presbyters prophesied to him. Then they prayed over him to seal the word. They sent him back to his seat, then went back into their huddle to find whom God wanted next. One of them stepped forth and called me to come forward. I knelt at a chair as they prayed and then started prophesying. All four of them prophesied to me. They then had me stand up and prophesy, which I did. Then they sent me back to my seat. They went back into their prayer huddle and came out and announced that they believed that was all the Holy Spirit wanted to do that night. The remaining 78 were so disappointed and discouraged that they all went to the altar and cried, moaned, and groaned for almost an hour. That was the only Prophetic Presbytery they had for the whole year.

I recorded the pages of prophecy that came over me in my first prophetic book, titled Prophets and Personal Prophecy. I recorded it for two reasons. First, for the younger generation to see what personal prophecy looked and sounded like in those days. At the time, there were hardly any Bibles in modern English. Most felt that prophecy had to sound like the English in the King James Bible. The prophetic presbytery became the way that personal prophecy was delivered to individuals. A prophet prophesying by himself to people was not acceptable to the leaders of the Latter Rain Movement, the ones who restored laying on of hands and prophecy back into the church.

In 1973, God launched me into a whole new dimension of personal prophecy to individuals. I was on a scheduled trip to the western states in the US. I stopped in Sacramento, California, where a young evangelist was conducting a three-week revival. He was a young man I had taught for a couple of years in Bible college. He told me he had felt inspired to tell the people that God wanted to speak to every one of them before the revival was over. He said to me, "Brother Hamon, I told the people this. I don't prophesy— you're the only one I know who prophesies to individuals, and now you show up here unexpectedly on the last night of the revival."

Back in 1964, when I first started teaching at the Bible college, I had prophesied to a young 17-year-old student that she would marry a preacher, and this young evangelist was the preacher she married. He asked if I would believe God to show me several people to prophesy to, because he had told them God wanted to speak to them.

It was 9:30 pm when I started calling people out and giving them personal prophecy. After ministering to about 15 saints, I felt I should probably close it out, for I had never seen more than 15-20 prophesied over in a prophetic presbytery meeting in one day. I felt a strong anointing and prophetic words for a few more, but when I reached the 20th person, I stopped prophesying because I had a mindset that 20 was a Holy Ghost maximum for one period of prophesying. So, I told the 85 people who were there to line up around the wall of the church so we could bring them through the blessing line for the ministers to lay hands on them. I was at the beginning of the blessing line. When I laid hands on the first person who came through the line, flashes of revelation illuminated my mind about this individual. The Lord was showing me what they were going through and what God's call was upon their life, as well as many other things. The anointing was boiling in my spirit like a volcano that was about to erupt. I thought I had already reached my quota and could not prophesy to anyone else, so I let them continue on through the line. The same thing happened with the next person, and then the third one. Flashes of revelation were flooding my mind, and my inner volcano felt like it was going to erupt.

I asked the Lord in my mind, "Why are you giving me these insights into these people's lives, and why such an anointing? Do you want me to prophesy over everyone you give me a word for?" He said, "Yes, my son. Open your mouth and speak the words and

When I laid hands on the first person who came through the line, flashes of revelation illuminated my mind about this individual. The anointing was boiling in my spirit like a volcano that was about to erupt.

visions I give you for everyone." So, when I laid hands on the next one, the flashes of revelation came and I opened my mouth. Personal prophesy flowed like a river. I ended up laying hands on everyone, and personal prophecy flowed to every single one. I finished with the 85th person at 2:30 in the morning. This was mystifying to me, for I had never heard or seen anyone prophesy continuously over scores of people.

When I arrived back home, I did endless research to see if I could find anyone who had ever done such a thing. I found no records in past history, but I did find in my book of personal prophecies where a young prophet whom I had trained in the prophetic had given me a prophecy in November of the previous year that stated that God was going to do a new thing in my life in which prophecy would flow out of me from one day into the next.

That night I had flowed in prophecy from 9:30 pm through midnight into the next day until 2:30 am. I thought that this was probably a one-time sovereign experience. But two weeks later, I was in Pennsylvania preaching to 150 people. After preaching, I started laying hands on people to pray for them, and instead of praying, prophecy flowed. At three o'clock in the morning, I finished with the 150th person. After that, for the next 20 years, I prophesied over everyone in churches of 300 or less in one or two nights. During those days when I was traveling in ministry, I averaged about 500 people a week. You can see why I was able to prophesy to more than 45,000 people during those years.

TRAINING MATERIALS FOR THE PROPHETIC

We moved Christian International headquarters from San Antonio, Texas, to Phoenix, Arizona, in 1977. That year, I started conducting a Friday night School of the Holy Spirit from 7:00 pm until after midnight, sometimes to 2:00 am. In 1983, we moved CI headquarters to the panhandle of Florida, where we started conducting Sons of the Prophet Seminars. These were two weeks of intensified prophetic training. I also started writing the prophetic book Prophets and Personal Prophecy. It was published in 1987. I couldn't find any publishers that would print the book because most churches did not believe there were prophets alive and active in the 20th century church. Destiny Image, a brand-new publishing company, was the only one willing to publish it, because they required the author to pay for the printing and then bought the books back from the author to distribute them. Prophets and Personal Prophecy was one of the first books that Destiny Image printed and distributed.

One of the reasons I'm sharing this is so you will understand why I did not have a mentor in this new flow of prophetic ministry; I was pioneering a brand new dimension of the prophetic. I continued writing books on the prophetic. My first book on The Eternal Church covered 500 years of church restoration. I noticed that moves of God that did not immediately birth books giving scriptural authority and validation to all that was happening didn't last very long, and erroneous teaching began to develop. The Prophetic Movement was birthed at our second "International Gathering of Apostles and Prophets" on October 15, 1988. I wrote the book *Prophets and the Prophetic Movement* to describe the ministry of the apostles and prophets, the 10 M's for discerning true and false prophets, and the 10 things the prophetic movement was restoring to the church that had not been restored in previous restoration movements. We then wrote the 300-page instruction manual for teaching in the prophetic schools and to give pastors the resources they needed to train their saints in prophetic ministry. After we started teaching and activating in prophetic seminars, we discovered that concerning the prophetic, Christians were like a bowl of cereal that had some flakes and nuts in it.

I then wrote my third book on the prophetic, titled *Prophets—Principles to Practice and Pitfalls to Avoid*. The first edition was printed in 1991. The second edition, published in 2021, has been updated and expanded with a new cover. In the 1980s, it was hard to find prominent ministers who would endorse a book on prophets and prophecy. But now, 30 years later, this second edition has a foreword written by Dr. Cindy Jacobs and endorsements by Chuck Pierce, Dutch Sheets, Lance Wallnau, Oral Roberts, James Goll, Apostle Guillermo Maldonado, Dr. Peter Wagner, Gordon Robertson of CBN, and Dr. Sharon Stone.

There are now millions of Christians and ministers who are endorsing and moving in prophetic ministry in all nations of the earth. Thank God, through the prophetic books and training manuals for ministering spiritual gifts, now there are three and four generations that have been affected by the prophetic and over one million who have prophesied or been ministered to by prophets. These include kings and queens of nations, people from every walk of life and all cultures and nations of the world. Nevertheless, the greatest ministry of the prophet is ahead of us. Prophecy is found in the Bible from the Garden of Eden to the last chapter of the Books of Revelation.

At the birthing of the Prophetic Movement, God lifted me into the heavenlies. Jesus approached me with a baby in His hands. He said, "This baby represents the Prophetic Movement that is being birthed tonight. Will you take a fathering role in helping Me raise My prophets to be the type of prophets I want representing Me in these last days? I am looking to them to make ready a people and prepare the way for Me to return and receive My bride-church." I said "yes" to His invitation, and that is why my ministry has been devoted all these years to raising up a company of prophets, a prophetic people who will sell out to Jesus Christ to be all He wants them to be. Those believers are willing to be the type of prophets and prophetic people required to reveal all mysteries and fulfill all things for His glorious return to earth

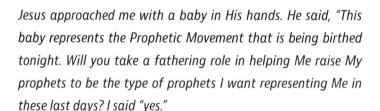

Jesus approached me with a baby in His hands. He said, "This baby represents the Prophetic Movement that is being birthed tonight. Will you take a fathering role in helping Me raise My prophets to be the type of prophets I want representing Me in these last days? I said "yes."

Jesus told me there would be 10,000 prophets and prophetic ministers on the North American continent and 100,000 in the rest of the continents of the World. I could hardly believe it, for in the early 1980s you could count on your fingers the number of prophets that were recognized as prophets of God. Prior to 1948, 99 percent of the church world did not believe there were prophets and apostles alive on planet Earth in the 20th century.

Jesus is very excited about His company of prophets who are now ministering on earth in the power and spirit of Elijah (Malachi 4:5, 6). When the Elijah prophet John the Baptist began ministering, Jesus knew His time to be the manifest son of God had arrived. In like manner, Jesus now beholds the great company of prophets actively preparing the way and making ready a people for His second coming.

Arise, prophets around the world, and reveal all the mysteries and fulfill all prophetic scriptures, which will release Jesus to come back as King of Kings and Lord of Lords to establish His Kingdom over all the earth,[1] *hastening the coming of the day of our God and Savior, Jesus Christ.*

---

1 (See Acts 3:21; Hebrews 10:13; Revelation. 10:7, 11:15; Daniel 7:22 and 3 Peter 3:12.)

Chapter Three

EMBRACING GOD'S HEART FOR LEGACY

Ché Ahn

Apostle/ President
Harvest International Ministry (HIM)
Pasadena, California

We serve a God of legacy. One of the key themes that resounds throughout Scripture is that God's heart is for family, and He is a God of generations. In Exodus 3:6, the Lord declares to Moses at the burning bush, "I am the God of your father—the God of Abraham, the God of Isaac, and the God of Jacob." The legacy we leave to our children—both in the natural and in the spirit—is tremendously important to God.

In my 48 years of walking with the Lord, family has played a central role as God the Father has moved powerfully in my life. Now as a father and grandpa, I am intentionally sowing into the next generations of my family by embracing the Father's heart. My wife, Sue, and I make it a priority to spend quality time with our kids and grandkids and to bless them with words of affection and affirmation. We also invest time in our spiritual children who live both locally and globally.

You may have heard it said, "As the family goes, so goes the nation." I believe now more than ever before that it is imperative for us to embody the biblical model for family. The world today is yearning for examples of healthy families.

Statistically speaking, we are living in the most fatherless generation ever. Every year since 2007, approximately 40% of births in the United States have been to a single parent. That is more than double the figures from the year 1980.[2] In the Hebrew mindset, most of the children being raised today are orphaned, as the Hebrew word for *orphan* means "fatherless."

In his 2008 Father's Day speech, President Obama painted a sobering picture of America's youth. Although I disagree with many of his policies and some of his values, I agree with what he said in this speech:

> Children who grow up without a father are five times more likely to live in poverty and commit crime; nine times more likely to drop out of schools, and twenty times more likely to end up in prison. They are more likely to have behavioral problems, or run away from home, or become teenage parents themselves. And the foundations of our community are weaker because of it.[3]

This statement, just as valid today, underscores the crucial role of being a parent who is present.

---

2 Frédéric Michas. "Percentage of births to unmarried women in the United States from 1980 to 2019." Statista. May 28, 2021. https://www.statista.com/statistics/276025/us-percentage-of-births-to-unmarried-women/

3 "Text of Obama's fatherhood speech." *Politico*. June 15, 2008. https://www.politico.com/story/2008/06/text-of-obamas-fatherhood-speech-011094

MALACHI 4:5-6 SEASON

I believe in this momentous chapter in history—we are in a Malachi 4:5-6 season. These two verses contain a prophetic promise that changed my life—and by God's grace, they will change yours, too:

> Behold, I am going to send you Elijah the prophet before the coming of the great and terrible day of the LORD. He will restore the hearts of the fathers to their children and the hearts of the children to their fathers, so that I will not come and smite the land with a curse. (Malachi 4:5-6 NASB95)

To understand the significance of this passage, we must first look at the life of Elijah in the Old Testament. Elijah is considered one of the two greatest prophets in Israel's history, Moses being the other. It is significant that both Moses and Elijah appeared before Jesus on the Mount of Transfiguration (see Matthew 17:1-3).

As 1 Kings chapters 17 and 18 recount, the prophet Elijah was a revivalist who brought revival to the Northern Kingdom of Israel, as they had become Baal worshipers under King Ahab and Queen Jezebel. As a side note, this is especially relevant today because I believe that the spirit of Jezebel is in our land like never before. But for the purpose of this chapter, let's focus on the question: *Why was Elijah chosen to exemplify God's heart for legacy?*

CALLED TO ANOINT THE NEXT GENERATION

To embrace God's heart for legacy, we would do well to look at the life of Elijah. One vital observation we must make is that *Elijah was chosen to anoint the next generation of leaders of his time.*

After an unforgettable showdown with the prophets of Baal on Mount Carmel, Elijah was on the run from Jezebel and devoid of hope for the future. Israel's mighty prophet found himself at the end of a 40-day journey to Mount Horeb, the mountain of God. Elijah was so discouraged that he was completely oblivious to an extremely important part of his calling that was yet unfulfilled. God was calling Elijah to raise up the next generation of leaders.

The word of the Lord came to him in a still, small voice and commissioned him with the following directives:

> Then the LORD said to him: 'Go, return on your way to the Wilderness of Damascus; and when you arrive, anoint Hazael as king over Syria. Also you shall anoint Jehu the son of Nimshi as king over Israel. And Elisha the son of Shaphat of Abel Meholah you shall anoint as prophet in your place. It shall be that whoever escapes the sword of Hazael, Jehu will kill; and whoever escapes the sword of Jehu, Elisha will kill. Yet I have reserved seven thousand in Israel, all whose knees have not bowed to Baal, and every mouth that has not kissed him.' (1 Kings 19:15-18 NKJV)

These were Elijah's marching orders: *Anoint the next generation.* While we often lend most of our attention to Elisha (and for good reason), I want to point out that God first told Elijah to anoint Hazael and Jehu as kings. God had serious plans for Israel as well as for Syria, and He knew that these two geopolitical leaders could be used as instruments for His divine purposes. Most notably, the anointed military leader Jehu would be the one to bring Jezebel to her end (see 2 Kings 9:30-33).

With this divine commission, Elijah left Mount Horeb with a new vision. The first thing he did was to find Elisha, and he threw his mantle over him. The late American evangelist Morris Cerullo writes of this prophetic exchange:

> The mantle … a rough, hairy garment … had come to be recognized as the garb of a prophet. It was a sign of the prophet's vocation. To cast his mantle upon Elisha was a significant way of designating him to the prophetic office. It meant his adoption as the spiritual son and successor of Elijah as a prophet of God over Israel.[4]

That day, Elisha left everything behind to serve the prophet Elijah. With this prophetic mantle now on his shoulders, Elisha was determined to receive the fullest impartation possible from his spiritual father. In their story of legacy, Elisha received a double portion of Elijah's anointing (see 2 Kings 2:9-14). Indeed, the Bible records that Elisha did twice the number of miracles as his mentor Elijah! Thus we can see God's desire for the next generation of leaders to do greater things.

ELIJAH'S TWOFOLD REVIVAL MANTLE

Yet Elijah's mantle didn't end there. In Malachi 4:5, God said that He was going to send the prophet Elijah before the great and terrible day of the Lord. My interpretation is that it is not the literal coming of Elijah but the prophetic mantle of Elijah, a revival spirit that will come twice in history.

First, the mantle came before the "great" day of the Lord, which was the first coming of Jesus. That anointing fell upon John the Baptist. As Gabriel prophesied to Zechariah concerning John:

---

4 Morris Cerullo. "Elisha was Called and Anointed." December 14, 2019. https://morriscerullo.com/elisha-was-called-and-anointed/

And he will go on before the Lord, *in the spirit and power of Elijah*, to turn the hearts of the parents to their children and the disobedient to the wisdom of the righteous—to make ready a people prepared for the Lord. (Luke 1:17 NIV)

After 400 years of silence, the prophetic voice of the Lord broke onto the scene in the Judean wilderness when John the Baptist emerged as a forerunner for the Messiah.

The Gospel of Matthew makes this explicitly clear in chapter 17, verses 10 through 13:

And His disciples asked Him, saying, 'Why then do the scribes say that Elijah must come first?' Jesus answered and said to them, 'Indeed, Elijah is coming first and will restore all things. But I say to you that Elijah has come already, and they did not know him but did to him whatever they wished. Likewise the Son of Man is also about to suffer at their hands.' Then the disciples understood that He spoke to them of John the Baptist. (NKJV)

Second, the mantle of Elijah will come before the "terrible" day of the Lord, the second coming of Christ. This is when He will judge the nations, separating the sheep from the goats (see Matthew 25). That second mantle is upon the Church. In the last days, I believe there will be a key prophetic company to prepare the way of the second coming of Jesus. As Christians, we don't believe in reincarnation, so we don't believe that John the Baptist was the reincarnation of Elijah. That is why my interpretation is that this is *the mantle* of Elijah coming on God's people.

REVIVAL AND RECONCILIATION

I believe that Malachi 4:5-6 reveals that fathers specifically—and spiritual parents more generally—are the key to historic revival.

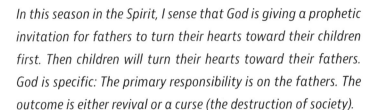

In this season in the Spirit, I sense that God is giving a prophetic invitation for fathers to turn their hearts toward their children first. Then children will turn their hearts toward their fathers. God is specific: The primary responsibility is on the fathers. The outcome is either revival or a curse (the destruction of society).

Scripture makes it clear that judgment begins in the house of the Lord (see 1 Peter 4:17). In this season in the Spirit, I sense that God is giving a prophetic invitation for fathers to turn their hearts toward their children first. Then children will turn their hearts toward their fathers. God is specific: The primary responsibility is on the fathers. The outcome is either revival or a curse (the destruction of society). That is why it is so important to have spiritual fathers and mothers who are actively seeking reconciliation as they shepherd the next generation.

The heart of Malachi 4:6—"He will restore the hearts of the fathers to their children and the hearts of the children to their fathers"—began to be realized in my life in 1994 during the Toronto Blessing outpouring, when I repented of bitter root judgments against my father. Even though my upbringing was rocky in many ways, I was blessed with two incredible parents who left behind legacies as a great man and woman of God.

One of the most impactful experiences in my life then came in 1996 when I received a blessing from my dad, and God brought reconciliation to our relationship. During a heart-to-heart conversation that I will never forget, my father asked for my forgiveness for the sins that he had committed against me when I was a child. Hearing my father say the words "I love you" for the first time in my life brought healing to my heart and released the power of a father's blessing, which has shaped my life and ministry ever since.

Malachi 4:6 later became the key verse for TheCall, a prayer movement that was birthed out of Harvest Rock Church through Lou Engle. One of the most powerful parts of the first solemn assembly was seeing parents and children getting reconciled and having a foot-washing time between natural parents or spiritual parents and their children. I believe that God allowed Lou and me to lead TheCall because our hearts embrace the value of legacy.

GENERATIONAL LEGACY: FROM GLORY TO GLORY

As Scripture shows us, the progression of Kingdom legacy is from glory to glory. We saw this with Elisha receiving the double portion from Elijah, but we as New Covenant believers are now living in another even greater promise. In Matthew 11:11, Jesus said that John the Baptist was the greatest prophet ever born to a woman, but now the least in the Kingdom—the least in the Church—is greater than John the Baptist. After all, this is God's heart for legacy: that the ceiling of the previous generation would be the floor for the next generation.

I saw firsthand God's heart for legacy exemplified with my late spiritual father and mentor, Dr. C. Peter Wagner. In 2010, Peter decided to give his three significant ministries to his spiritual children. He gave Global Harvest to Chuck Pierce, who changed the name to Global Spheres. He gave the Reformation Prayer Network and the Prophetic Roundtable to Cindy Jacobs. And Peter gave me his seminary, Wagner Leadership Institute (now Wagner University).

It is a true honor to carry on part of the spiritual legacy of this amazing man of God.

Raising Up Spiritual Sons and Daughters

As the years go by, I have become more cognizant of my need to pour into the next generation. The Holy Spirit has been showing me that the way the Father's blessing is going to be restored is by raising up godly fathers and mothers. This is the word that Cindy Jacobs gave me in the 1990s, that I would be like Abraham and be a father of many. By God's grace, today I am privileged to have spiritual children all around the world.

Around eight years ago, I saw the shift happening globally when people started to call me "Papa Ché." Although I wasn't a fan of the word "Papa" at first, it dawned upon me that I am a grandfather. My heart started to realize that I needed to be more intentional about being a spiritual father. Soon enough, "Papa Ché" became a term of endearment. I have grown to like it because it is an honoring term while still being informal.

Looking back at my book *Modern-Day Apostles*, something I would have emphasized more strongly was the truth that apostles are spiritual fathers. The apostle Paul writes to the church in Corinth, "For though you might have ten thousand instructors in Christ, yet you do not have many fathers; for in Christ Jesus I have begotten you through the gospel" (1 Corinthians 4:15). Peter Wagner once said, "You're not a success unless you have a successor." I cannot agree more.

In recent years, one of the ways Sue and I have been intentionally pouring into the younger generation is through our annual School of the Apostles (SOA). Each year, we carve out a few days from our schedule to disciple and develop emerging apostolic leaders that we know personally. Even when I have the opportunity to preach to thousands of people at a time, I honestly feel more fulfilled ministering and sharing life with a smaller group. I say that because we see great value in the lasting quality of these relationships: discipling Christ followers and guiding them to walk into their divine destinies.

I believe the Word of God instructs fivefold leaders to mentor others in their Ephesians 4:11 calling. In other words, equip leaders in the same sphere you are called to. For example, my goal is to raise up other apostles with SOA. This is one of the creative ways in which leaders can mentor the next generation. It could be a "School of Evangelists" for someone in the office of an evangelist, a "School of Prophets" for those in that office, and so forth.

While hosting events like these is important, mentoring is also an organic part of developing the relationships in my life. I have spiritual sons and daughters who I am regularly investing time in. Some of these are pastors in our church, most of whom are Millennials. I thank God for the quality of leaders that He has placed in our midst; it's incredible how teachable they are.

One of the Harvest Rock pastors I want to highlight is my spiritual son Jay Koopman. This is a man with whom I have had a relationship for over 20 years. Jay has served as my Associate Pastor and the leader of our satellite campus in Orange County. As of the writing of this book, I have released Jay to travel with Sean Feucht and the Let Us Worship movement that has impacted over 133 cities across America. Jay has led thousands to the Lord in this current move of the Spirit. It has been so encouraging to see God working mightily through him.

And not only in the church—I am also raising up marketplace leaders who God is calling to transform their mountain of culture—whether in business, government, family, education, arts and entertainment, or media.

THE RESTORATION OF THE FATHER'S HEART

Ultimately, the way we move as spiritual children—directly receiving the love of the Father—reflects the way we will move as spiritual parents. When we lead our lives centered on God's love, the culture around us will be transformed, as *the hearts of the fathers turn to the children, and the hearts of the children to their fathers* (Malachi 4:6).

The way you lead your family, business, or ministry will have a direct impact on the world, as the next generation will be in your shoes soon enough! The way we instill biblical values in the lives of our physical and spiritual children and the way we consistently demonstrate our faith through our actions will set the following generations on the right path and lead them to success.

Our responsibility and joy as parents and leaders is to sow into our families—relationally, spiritually, even financially—knowing that our seeds will enable our children to see greater things and reap

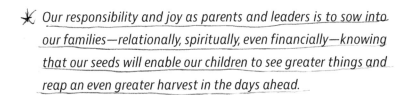

Our responsibility and joy as parents and leaders is to sow into our families—relationally, spiritually, even financially—knowing that our seeds will enable our children to see greater things and reap an even greater harvest in the days ahead.

an even greater harvest in the days ahead. Being a spiritual father or mother to the next generation is part of our calling to be salt and light to a world that is longing for the truth of Jesus Christ.

I believe the restoration of the Father's heart to society is a manifestation of the Revival that is emerging all across the globe. Each one of us was created to receive the love of the Father and to live a life marked by the Father's blessing. If you belong to Christ, you are an ambassador of His radical love. And wherever He is sending you in the world, Abba God wants you to win souls and disciple spiritual children into maturity in His Kingdom.

Today I commission you to speak destiny into the next generation as fathers and mothers who carry the Father's heart!

Chapter Four

ELIJAH/ELISHA - JOINING THE GENERATIONS

Jane Hamon

Co-pastor
Vision Church at Christian International
Santa Rosa Beach, Florida

A few years ago, I was flying home from a ministry trip on a flight from Los Angeles to Atlanta. I had just been upgraded to first class when a young, hip-looking black man sat down next to me while talking on his phone. I couldn't help but overhear his conversation, which sounded like a negotiation for a movie deal. When he got off the phone, he apologized for being loud in his conversation, and we began to talk. I found out he was a movie producer in Hollywood, with several recognizable titles, and a consultant for clothing stores who helped set the upcoming trends. He was quite influential with the younger generation.

After we talked about him for quite a while, he asked me what I did for a living. I told him I was a minister—a pastor—in the church. He shook his head and said, "Hmmm, I have never had much use for the church. Sorry." I truly don't think he was trying to be disrespectful, because our conversation was friendly. He just seemed to feel the church was completely irrelevant to his life.

I responded, "So you aren't very interested in religion, huh? Well, neither am I." He turned and looked at me with surprise. I went on, "You see, in many places today, the church doesn't really act like who Jesus wanted us to be. I believe if you knew the kind of church Jesus gave His life for, you wouldn't be indifferent—instead you wouldn't be able to resist us!" He was intrigued and a bit shocked by my answer, so he turned and faced me and said, "Well, we've got lots of time on this flight. Why don't you explain to me what the real church is supposed to look like and why I should care?" Wow! What an open door!

I spent the next five hours talking to him about who Jesus was, who the Church was supposed to be, and how the Lord wanted to change his life. He said he felt this was the answer he was looking for because he really needed a change in his life. When I asked him why he felt that way, he said, "Easy! I became a father! It is changing everything about me." At the end of the flight we prayed together, and he received Jesus as his Savior.

Before we deplaned, he commented once again that he knew he needed to change his life because even though he had success with his career, money, and fame, he recognized some of the movies he produced contained pretty rough content. He realized since he had become a dad himself that he didn't want those movies influencing his own children as they grew up, let alone his kid's generation. He felt giving his life to the Lord would help him become the kind of dad he wanted to be. He wanted to be connected to his kids in a better way than he ever was to his own parents.

This conversation stuck with me for years. I realized that the younger generation was hungry for connection and for real relationship with Jesus, not just another religion. They are looking for that which is life-giving and authentic which can help them be better people, better parents, and better leaders for tomorrow. They are looking for a church that demonstrates power and also walks with integrity. They are looking for relatable leaders who are bold and full of faith, who believe miracles still happen today, and who are willing to lay down their lives to make a way for others to experience everything Jesus died to bring us.

The current emerging generation has some of the biggest challenges to face. Statistically, one third of the generation of those who would be graduating from high school today were aborted. This breeds a culture of death which subconsciously communicates that life has little value. No wonder kids are killing other kids in our schools and in our cities. Parents in this generation can decide to kill their own baby in the womb with no stigma or conviction, as they've been told it is not really a life. Many in this generation are being brought up by single parents in broken homes, often with a revolving door of partners. Some have never seen an example of a good, healthy marriage, which only sets them up for future broken homes and children without two parents. This is the first generation that now asks the question: *Am I really a man or a woman, a boy or a girl, or some other combination of genders? Do I marry a man or a woman? Who am I really?* This generation is crying out for mothers and fathers who will speak true Christ-given identity to them. They are looking for those to give structure and meaning to their lives, to lead them to Christ, and to speak destiny and purpose into them. They are looking for those who will prepare the way before them to

This generation is crying out for mothers and fathers who will speak true Christ-given identity to them ... They are looking for those who will prepare the way before them to help them become who God created them to be and to fulfill their God-given purpose in life.

help them become who God created them to be and to fulfill their God-given purpose in life.

For those who are reading this book, I believe they are looking for us! You may be a leader seeking a deeper understanding of how to build with upcoming generations; how to effectively inspire them, teach, train, and activate them in their gifts and callings in Christ. Or perhaps you are someone looking for a leader who will model success in life, marriage, family, and ministry, and who will provide opportunity for you to grow into a good leader yourself. Welcome to the Elijah/Elisha journey! It will take the joining of the generations to cause the next great awakening, the greatest revival to hit planet earth—the incredible last days harvest of billions of souls.

ELIJAHS AND ELISHAS

When I was sixteen years old, I heard the audible voice of God instruct me to go to Bible college and call me into full-time ministry. He told me I would meet a man at college, we would get married young, and then He would thrust us into the ministry. We would travel the nations of the world. Sometimes he would preach, and sometimes I would preach, because we would be a team in ministry.

You have to understand that God spoke this to me in 1978 when the concept of husband and wife ministry teams was quite foreign in the church; and in most circles, women didn't preach. Yet, a year later, I headed off to Christ for the Nations, where I met Tom Hamon my first day on campus. We were married two years later and planted our first church two months later. He was twenty-one, and I was nineteen. We were so young! But we were passionate about serving God together in ministry, even though we weren't sure what we were doing or what that would look like.

Thank God for Tom's dad and mom, Bill and Evelyn Hamon. If the name sounds familiar, it's because he is known as the "father of the modern day prophetic movement." He has written fourteen books and many manuals on training up prophets and has trained over 500,000 people all over the world with his materials. However, when Tom and I got married, he was just operating as a prophet in ministry but had not yet begun training up prophets. We were privileged to be among some of the first whom he trained and raised up, not only to prophesy, but also to operate under the anointing of prophets and leaders in the Body of Christ.

He was our Elijah: urging us to grow, challenging us to be even bolder than he was, pressing us to step out of our comfort zone and be activated in our gifts. When we felt we weren't ready to step into a new prophetic challenge, he would put a demand on what was inside us and push us forward. Yet, at the same time, he was always encouraging us with his own life stories and example. He modeled for us how to live our lives, raise our family in ministry, and handle lack, hardship, rejection, offense, and difficulties so that we could overcome any kind of adversity along life's path. He was a forerunner, a pioneer in prophetic ministry who withstood persecution, not from the world but from his fellow ministers in Christ who doubted he could do what he did. He ran hard, yet he would tell us he expected us to accomplish more than he did in ministry. He was never going to stop, so we would need to run hard to catch up with him and surpass him.

We have now been in full-time ministry for over forty years together and have traveled to over sixty-five nations. Sometimes Tom preaches, and sometimes I preach. We are a team. Together we have pioneered and overseen an apostolic/prophetic church for over thirty-five years. I was also a forerunner as a strong woman in ministry. Now there are many husband/wife teams in ministry, as well as many strong, anointed women preachers. We have developed teaching and training for a new generation of prophets with our *School of the Prophets 90 Day Intensive*. Now there aren't just a few prophets here and there, but an entire company of prophets throughout the earth from several generations.

Now, *we* are the Elijahs to younger, upcoming Elishas, who are full of passion and the zeal of the Lord but have so many challenges to overcome to be all God has called them to be. We are now modeling for them what it takes to be in ministry, to have a strong marriage, to raise godly children, to hear the voice of the Lord, to interpret dreams and visions and to be prophets to the nations, as well as how to bring territorial transformation through strategic intercession and prophetic decrees. We run hard but are full of joy in our service, exemplifying a passionate and purposeful life and ministry for our Elishas.

This obviously didn't happen overnight. In order to become good Elijahs, we had to first learn what it was to be a good Elisha. Here are some characteristics that we've found to be marks of emerging Elishas:

1. A Servant's Heart

Elisha was described as being "one that poured water on the hands of Elijah" or as "Elijah's servant." In our early days of ministry, we did whatever our hands found to do to support our Elijah in ministry. It really wasn't about us or "our ministry," but about making him a success through our service, as well as building that which he was building and taking on whatever assignment he gave us. Sometimes that meant working for very little pay (or none at all) since the ministry was still in its pioneering stage, or collating courses by hand in a back room. Sometimes it meant doing set up and tear down at conferences, or prophesying to people until the wee hours of the morning, because one man couldn't do it all. We served with our gifts, both natural and spiritual, and did it with a good heart. We didn't believe we were entitled to position or opportunity just because we were Elishas (nor because we were the actual son and daughter-in-law of our leader). We believed that as we served and were faithful, God would promote us in due season. We learned that a mantle cannot be grasped; a mantle must be passed, with intention and impartation. We knew our faithfulness would pave the way for future positioning and power, not just before men, but before God.

2. Perseverant

Elisha had to choose to pursue Elijah, and Elijah often didn't seem to make it easy for him! When God spoke to Elijah to anoint

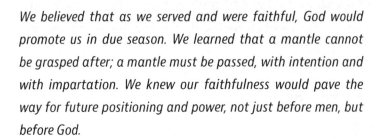

We believed that as we served and were faithful, God would promote us in due season. We learned that a mantle cannot be grasped after; a mantle must be passed, with intention and with impartation. We knew our faithfulness would pave the way for future positioning and power, not just before men, but before God.

Elisha to be his successor, Elisha was a successful businessman with twelve yoke of oxen. Elijah walked by and threw his mantle onto Elisha, which signified he was being called to follow Elijah. Elisha responded, "Let me kiss my father and mother, and then I will follow you. And he [testing Elisha] said, 'Go on back. What have I done to you? [Settle it for yourself]'" (1 Kings 19:20 AMPC). This seemed a bit harsh to my way of communicating; however, we see that Elisha responded by cooking the oxen and feeding others with the meat, then running after Elijah.

We don't see anything of Elisha again until 2 Kings 2 when Elijah is getting ready to be taken to Heaven in a whirlwind. As the two of them travel together, Elijah visits three of the cities that have a company of prophets, which Bible scholars identify as schools of the prophets. Three times they visit prophets, and three times the prophets tell Elisha that his master will be taken away from him that day. Three times Elijah encourages Elisha to stop following him and to stay with the other prophets. This certainly could have felt like rejection; however, each time Elisha responds by saying, "I am not staying, and I am not letting you out of my sight!"

If one is the Elisha in relationship with an Elijah, you must be prepared to persevere past disappointment, unrealized expectations, and offense. Those who are serving as Elijahs are only human and will make mistakes. They may be more focused on the weighty assignments of the Lord than on the relational needs of their Elishas. From our experience, the best way to build relationally with our Elijah was to shoulder up and work with him. It wasn't all about the work, however; it was about building relationship while carrying responsibility together. We had to learn not to get our feelings hurt if he corrected us, or even if we disagreed with him. We learned to get our hearts right quickly and get back to Kingdom business. If we had an opportunity to talk things through with him to help bring resolve, great. If not, we moved forward and persevered through our difficulty until inner peace and unity came.

3. Boldness to Ask for More

When the time came for Elijah to be taken away from Elisha, Elisha was perseverant to not leave his side, for this was the moment when he knew he would receive an inheritance. The Bible never says whether or not Elijah ever told Elisha that God had spoken to him that he would be his successor. We are never told if Elisha ever prophesied or did any kind of prophetic act before this time. However, Elisha learned by watching Elijah, and somewhere along the line he knew he wanted what Elijah had. So when the moment came, and Elijah asked him, "What shall I do for you before I am taken away from you?" Elisha knew exactly what he wanted: "Please let a double portion of your spirit be upon me." He wanted to walk in even more power and anointing than what Elijah walked in. He wanted to accomplish more miracles than Elijah accomplished. He boldly asked for a double portion.

Again, Elijah didn't make granting this request easy for Elisha. He told him he was asking for something that was very hard. It wasn't just a difficult ask; it would mean a difficult and challenging life. But he told Elisha that if he kept his eyes on him when he was taken away, he could have the mantle and all that entailed. "If you see me when I am taken away from you, it shall be so, but if you don't see me, it shall not be so." In his final act of mentoring, he was telling Elisha not to lose his focus.

I preached a message one time on focus and used this word to represent our faith positioning: "Faith Operating Consistently Until Satisfied." This is what it will take for us to follow in the footsteps of Christ, who told us we would do greater things than He did because He was going to His Father. Elijah laid the foundation through his supernatural lifestyle; Elisha did double the miracles.

Sometimes as an Elisha, we just needed our Elijah to help us keep things in perspective so we won't lose our focus. In time of heartbreak, trials, and even betrayal, our Elijah walked us through and helped us keep our hearts right and our perspective clear.

4. Honor

When Elijah was taken up into Heaven through the whirlwind, Elisha cried out, "My father, my father, the chariots of Israel and its horsemen." Elisha loved Elijah as a son loved his father and wanted

---

What we have received today is far greater than the double portion mantle of Elijah! We have received the very mantle of Christ by the indwelling of the Holy Spirit!

---

to honor him. Elijah's mantle fell down and Elisha picked it up. This is such a picture of what happened when Jesus ascended to Heaven in His resurrected body, having defeated death, hell, and the grave. Jesus went up and His mantle came down in the form of Holy Spirit. Elijah's mantle was a double portion mantle, whereas the Holy Spirit mantle contained nine gifts and nine fruit of the Spirit and the five-fold ministry gifts of apostle, prophet, evangelist, pastor and teacher. What we have received today is far greater than the double portion mantle of Elijah! We have received the very mantle of Christ by the indwelling of the Holy Spirit!

When Elisha picked up the mantle, he went back to the same Jordan River that Elijah had parted and did exactly what he had seen Elijah do. He rolled up the mantle and struck the water, crying out, "Where is the Lord God of Elijah?" Elijah's last miracle became Elisha's first miracle. He was picking up where Elijah left off just as we were intended to pick up where Jesus left off. When Elisha made this declaration, he was honoring his spiritual father but at the same time making his own personal connection to the God of Elijah. While Elijah was on earth, Elisha honored him with his service. After his departure, he honored Elijah by remembering everything he had ever been taught and every example Elijah ever set for him. Elisha had a different ministry than Elijah, but the example Elijah set for him was present in every daring miracle, every righteous challenge to kings, and every supernatural act. He picked up where Elijah left off and his life of honor paved the way for his success.

You can never go wrong honoring your predecessor. God loves honor, which connects the generations.

ELIJAHS, ARISE!

The Bible doesn't tell us if Elijah was ever mentored by anyone. It appears that he began as a lone prophet, raised in obscurity until his debut in I Kings 17 when he calls for the heavens to be shut up and not produce rain. We mostly see him operating alone in Scripture. However, we know he raised up at least three companies of prophets, for these were the places he visited before his miraculous departure. We know God chose Elisha, and Elijah allowed him, above others, to travel with him, serve him, and be directly mentored by him through the life he exampled so he could be his successor.

Through our over 40 years of ministry, God has brought us many strong leaders, some who were Elijahs themselves, already trained and skilled, and others who were Elishas being raised up. We learned early on that to be good leaders who would reproduce strong leaders, we needed to exemplify the ministry and character traits found in the life of Elijah. Here are some of the components for a successful Elijah lifestyle, which would then of course, also be reproduced in the lives of the Elishas.

1. Passionate Prayer

James 5:16-17 tells us of Elijah's effectual, fervent prayer life. He prayed, and the heavens were shut up; then he prayed again, and it rained. Our prayer life is that which catapults us into a supernatural lifestyle. Elijahs should model a life of prayer to their Elishas. Tom and I believe in living lives of personal prayer as well as corporate prayer. Out of those times, we have released prophetic words and decrees that have shifted our lives, our land, and our region.

On one occasion, we had been experiencing a severe drought in our area. God gave me a prophetic word in prayer one day that, like Elijah, declared, "I hear the sound of the abundance of rain," We were to declare the same over our region. I heard this in personal prayer, and we carried it into corporate prayer that evening, decreeing what God had said. Three days later, the heavens opened, and it rained for several days straight, causing the scientists to declare, "The drought is over!"

Elishas with whom we have shared this story receive a revelation about what is possible when one hears from Heaven and decrees it into the earth, giving them courage to walk this out in their own journey.

2. Willing to Pioneer

Elijah did powerful prophetic acts throughout his ministry, and most of the time we see him going it alone. Though his later years, he was connected to companies of prophets and to Elisha; he had to be willing to obey God all by himself, if necessary, and to do things no one had ever done before. God's heart is to connect each of us to a company of prophets; however, there will be times in each of our lives when God may bring a revelation or an assignment that is unusual or not modeled by others. God wants to give each of us the courage to pioneer new areas and new ministries and to break open new pathways so others can follow in our footsteps. However, the day of the one man show is over, so even in our pioneering, it is important to connect with others.

3. Boldness to Confront

Elijah's entire ministry was about confronting the evil of his generation to turn the people back to serving the one true God. He walked in great authority when confronting unrighteous King

Ahab. He exampled holy boldness as he had a confrontational showdown with the false prophets of Baal on Mount Carmel. He demonstrated unwavering strength when he executed the prophets of Baal and Ashtoroth, risking the anger of Queen Jezebel. He confronted death when he raised the widow's son from his death bed. It may almost seem like Elijah was always looking for a fight! But just like John the Baptist, who in the spirit and power of Elijah went about crying, "Prepare the way of the Lord; make straight paths," so Elijah knew his assignment could never be accomplished by being tolerant of the wickedness in the land.

In the same way, Elijahs must hold a righteous standard at a time in the earth when much of the church refuses to call sin "sin. We cannot afford to water down God's word. The Elishas we raise up must have a love for God's word and an uncompromising view of sin without being caught up in the compromise and tolerance of modern culture. God desires a company of prophets and leaders who have a holy boldness, yet are filled with grace and the power to set men and women free.

4. Understood Divine Provision

Elijah prophesied a drought that also affected him. He experienced times when God sent ravens to feed him by the brook supernaturally, and other times God sent him to people to provide for him, such as the widow at Zarephath. Not only did God unlock provision for him, but God used him to unlock provision for the widow and her entire household.

It's important for Elijahs to recount the stories of supernatural divine provision and encourage the upcoming generation that what He did for us, He will also do for them. Tom and I have shared with our Elishas so many testimonies about God's hand of provision for our lives, from school tuitions supernaturally being paid, to basic needs being met, to vacations being paid for, to God opening Heaven to provide a supernatural down payment for our house. These testimonies are more than just encouragements but actually bring the faith to unlock provision for themselves. It is an act of mentoring in how to believe God through impossible situations. He gives us a vision to fulfill, then brings the pro-vision to make it happen.

5. Made the Supernatural Natural

Elijah's life and ministry were marked by many usual miracles. His prophetic decrees initiated a drought, then, three and a half years later, brought the rain. He called down fire from Heaven. He raised the dead. He decreed, and the widow's oil and flour did not run out, all through the drought. He even beat death by being taken up into Heaven in a whirlwind and chariot of fire.

And standing on the ground watching Elijah beat death was Elisha, who understood he was being mantled with this same power to destroy death and all its emissaries. Elijah made it look easy. Elijah made the supernatural a natural part of his life, so Elisha

Throughout Scripture we see examples of generational continuity. God gave Abraham a vision of a nation coming out of his loins, but it took generations to fulfill it. God gave Moses the vision of the promised land, but Joshua took it. God gave David a dream of building Him a house, but Solomon built it.

could do the same. Elisha's decrees opened barren wombs, raised a dead son back to life, called down she-bears to destroy his enemies, caused a widow's oil to multiply, confronted kings, healed poisoned stew, cleansed a general of leprosy and on and on. Even after death, a dead man thrown on Elisha's bones jumped back to life!

Elijahs and Elishas alike are being challenged to do similar supernatural acts. We have told the stories of the sick we have prayed for who have been healed, the dead we have raised, hurricanes that have turned or dissipated because of our decrees, barren wombs opened, supernatural provision, and more. In Hebrew, the word for testimony means, "repeat, do it again." Each time we tell the stories, we open the heavens to see God do it again. It's time we make the supernatural natural again.

6. Generational Synergy

Elijah and Elisha modeled generational synergy...one generation connecting to another so that each generation can accomplish more. As amazing as Elijah's life was, his end would have been anti-climactic had there not been an Elisha to carry on his work. We know that God is a multigenerational God, identifying Himself as the God of Abraham, Isaac, and Jacob.

Throughout Scripture, we see examples of generational continuity. God gave Abraham a vision of a nation coming out of his loins, but it took generations to fulfill it. God gave Moses the vision of the promised land, but Joshua took it. God gave David a dream of building Him a house, but Solomon built it.

God always speaks vision for the upcoming generation. Josiah was anointed king at eight years old and was overthrowing altars of Baal by eighteen. Samuel was only a boy when God spoke to him prophetically about Eli's reprobate sons. Both David and Joseph received their callings to greatness at the age of seventeen, changing the course of their lives to work with God's process for fulfillment.

As a matter of fact, God has used one generation to break through to benefit the other. When Moses faced the Amalekites in battle, he stood on a mountain with the rod in his lifted hands. Joshua fought in the valley with the sword. Whenever Moses became weary and the rod in his hands dropped, Joshua got pushed back. Whenever his hands were lifted, Joshua prevailed. Joshua needed Moses' rod, but Moses also needed Joshua's sword and the hands of Aaron and Hur to keep him strong and see the victory.

When David killed Goliath, not only did he get to marry the king's daughter and move into the palace, but David's father also got the benefit of no longer having to pay taxes. In Esther's case, her uncle Mordecai instructed her and positioned her, working behind the scenes to set her up for success, but ultimately God's favor was upon her, and she won the heart of the king. Her favor then opened the door for not only Haman's decree of death and destruction to be turned on his own head, but also for Mordecai to step into a position of favor. Generational synergy—generations working together—saved a nation.

As we are in a new and exciting day of building generationally, we are seeing a new understanding of generations running together. The old model was for a leader to pass a mantle to his successor at retirement or just before he died—then the younger generation would run with a new leadership mandate. Today, however, we are seeing something new and exciting: Elijahs and Elishas running together. It's not only about generational continuity but about the power of synergy when we work together.

In our ministry, our Elijah, Bishop Bill Hamon, is still alive and active in ministry, even in his late 80s now. We serve alongside him, and our daughter and her husband serve alongside us. Now their daughter is on the worship team and pursuing the Lord through her youth group. We have four generations running together, sharpening one another, building one another, and being a blessing to one another. What a blessing to model Psalms 145:4, which says, "One generation shall praise Your works to another, and shall declare Your mighty acts."

7. A Curse Destroyer and Nation Changer

Elisha called Elijah "My father, my father" when he saw him taken to Heaven.

> Behold, I will send you Elijah the prophet before the coming of the great and dreadful day of the Lord. And he will turn the hearts of the fathers to the children, and the hearts of the children to their fathers, lest I come and strike the earth with a curse. (Malachi 4:5-6 NKJV)

Elijah was raised up to turn a nation back to the heart of God, to break them free of the curse that comes with idolatry, witchcraft, and sin. He knew that God's divine purposes could only be accomplished when fathers turned their hearts toward the upcoming generation, speaking identity to them, guiding them in the ways of God, and giving them courage to walk out their destiny. In turn, the hearts of the emerging generation would respond and thrive, and the curse of generational disconnection and fatherlessness would be broken. The devil is terrified of generations running together, for this always produces revival. He constantly strives to drive a wedge of division, misunderstanding, and judgment between the generations. However, God worked with Elijah, demonstrating signs and wonders to emphasize the authority with which he spoke and opened the hearts of another generation of prophets to arise and fulfill their assignment.

John the Baptist did the same as a younger generation, thirty-one year old forerunner. The religious spirit hates generational synergy and will always try to build a wall of division between those of differing ages and stages. Once the curse of disconnection is broken, anything can happen!

Elisha understood the power of the curse-breaking anointing, for the first thing he did after receiving Elijah's mantle was to part the river, cross over, and break the curse off Jericho which was under a famine at the time. He did a prophetic act, decreeing "no more death or barrenness," and healed the water of the city. Not only was the water healed, but the land, economy, families, crops, and flocks were healed, and God's name was glorified.

Jesus said it this way, "Behold, I give you power to tread on serpents and scorpions, and over all the power of the enemy and nothing shall by any means harm you." He was telling them, "You are my voice in the earth. Your assignment is to go out there and preach the good news of freedom in Christ, healing from sickness, deliverance from demonic oppression, and victory over every curse."

As we run together, generation to generation, older and younger, men and women, apostles and prophets, Africans, Hispanics, Asians, Caucasians, those called to pulpit ministry and those called to the workplace or government, we will see the fullness of the double-portion mantle manifested in our generation. Elijahs must turn their hearts to the Elishas, knowing they bring a fire, passion, and zeal. Elishas must turn their hearts to the Elijahs, knowing they bring wisdom, strategy, experience and courage. *When we run together, hearts joined to hearts, anything can happen!*

———— ⤷⤶⤸ ————

Chapter Five

MY JOURNEY WITH A GENERAL

Ryan LeStrange

Founder and Apostolic Leader
The TRIBE Network
Atlanta, Georgia

T he term "general" has become a buzzword to honor preachers and leaders, but I think we tend to overuse it and have taken something very special and made it extremely common. This, however, was not the case with my journey.

I was not raised in church, nor did I have family members who were active in ministry. In fact, on my Dad's side of the family, everyone that I knew was unchurched, and on my Mom's side, they were Catholic. This left me without an awareness of the gospel message of salvation by faith.

I was raised in a broken home with a lot of pain from addiction and bondage. I still remember the intense struggles of my childhood and young adulthood well. It seemed as though I was stuck in a never-ending cycle of pain, despair, and hopelessness. At a very young age, I came to know fear and pain in a life-altering way. This was the backdrop of my salvation.

I had an uncle who had been radically born again. My Catholic family was trying to figure out what that actually meant! *How does one become born again? Can a man be born a second time?* Does this sound familiar?

> Jesus answered and said unto him, "Verily, verily, I say unto thee, except a man be born again, he cannot see the kingdom of God." Nicodemus saith unto him, "How can a man be born when he is old? Can he enter the second time into his mother's womb, and be born?" (John 3:3-4 KJV)

Nicodemus was struggling with the concept of being born a second time. He was thinking of the natural birth, but Jesus was speaking of a spiritual birth. This was the state of mind that my family was in over my uncle being born again. All we knew is that his life was remarkably and wonderfully transformed. I was very close to him, as he became like a second father to me. Eventually, he invited me to his church and I was excited to go. I attended several times and had never experienced anything like it. It was a Word of Faith megachurch filled with life, excitement, and lengthy Bible teaching. One Sunday, the pastor shared the gospel message in a way that penetrated my young, broken heart, and I found myself responding to his call to be born again. The next thing I knew, I was at the altar receiving Jesus and then in the back room receiving the Holy Spirit! My life was forever changed that day. There were bumps in the road, and it would take some dramatic highs and lows before I finally surrendered, but I was on my way.

My uncle became my spiritual mentor and teacher during my growth process. I hit some significant lows before really selling out to God. When I went full throttle, I began to consume teaching. My uncle had a massive library of books and tapes (yes, I said tapes… some of you are too young to know, and others remember them well). I listened to nearly every Word of Faith teacher you could think of. One in particular stood out to me—a General named Norvel Hayes. He spoke with an authority I had never heard and didn't hear in the other teachers I would listen to. He talked about healing the sick in services that went past midnight and casting demons out of people who had lost their minds. I never had heard such supernatural stories in my life, nor had I ever heard a preacher talk with such boldness and audacious faith.

I was more than intrigued! His voice caused a deep stirring in my spirit, although I had no clue that was what I was experiencing. I was sitting in a service one day when I suddenly heard the voice of the Lord speak to me. You may ask, Did you hear the audible voice of God? The answer is, I am not really sure. All I know is that it was vivid, real, and weighty. The Lord said to me: "I have called you." I was honestly in shock and looked around, sure that God was talking to someone else. My dark childhood experiences had opened the door for such bondage and despair in my mind that I just knew God could not use me. It's sad to say that is where my mind was, but it is the absolute truth. I literally believed that God could use anyone but me. I have since come to realize it is often those cracked vessels that learn to pour the oil the best!

I questioned the Lord and even tried to negotiate with Him, telling Him I would be a good church member, teacher, and worker but *Please, Lord, don't call me to preach*. My mind was raging during that service as I tried to figure out who God was talking to. But He was clearly speaking to me and I knew it. The call of God was showing up in that moment, and I was being marked for a global destiny, but I was reluctant. I felt ill-equipped and unable to navigate the call to ministry. Even though I was so reluctant, I accepted the fact that God was calling me, and I made a decision that day to obey God. But I knew that I had to be trained. I decided then and there that I would go to Bible college, and I committed to pray about where to go and when. (*Side note:* I told God I would not do three things. I said I wouldn't preach, wouldn't go to Bible college and wouldn't move out of California where I was raised. I was particularly opposed to moving to the South. Don't get mad at me, all my southern friends! I was just a West Coast guy all the way. It's hilarious to me now because God had me do all three. You cannot direct your own ship if you are going to obey God!)

I kept listening to Dr. Hayes' tapes, and I heard him say he had a Bible college. Then and there I knew that was where I was supposed to go. I reached out to the school and sent in my application. My plan was to go in several months, but to make a very long story short, I ended up there in a matter of weeks. God accelerated the timing on everything and perfectly arranged it. In no time at all, I was packed and leaving California for Cleveland, Tennessee, to sit under the tutelage of the one who would shape the course of my destiny and become my spiritual father.

When I arrived at the school, I received major deliverance the very first day from Dr. Hayes' daughter, Zona, as she prayed for me. The atmosphere at the school was intense. I had never seen such spiritual hunger or experienced such authoritative teaching. The atmosphere was charged with unusual faith.

"Now faith is the assurance of things hoped for, the conviction of things not seen." (Hebrews 11:1 ESV)

One lesson I learned about journeying with great spiritual leaders is that there is a level of resistance from the enemy that you must discern and conquer in prayer.

We were being taught the power of faith and standing on God's Word. We learned that miracles are the result of faith. On that very first day, the devil tried to talk me into quitting because I was embarrassed about the deliverance I had received. I had to get real with God and make a decision not to let my pride block my hunger. One lesson I learned about journeying with great spiritual leaders is that there is a level of resistance from the enemy you must discern and conquer in prayer.

As my time continued there, I would sit in Dr. Hayes' sessions and learn so much about faith, deliverance, and the power of God. He was a humble but confident man who mostly taught by sharing scriptures and stories. He did not preach short sermons. In fact, the very first time I heard him preach, I thought the offering message was his entire sermon! I was packing up my Bible and notebook when one of the other students told me he was just getting warmed up. He used to say you cannot rush God. He moved slowly and reverentially as he ministered. Quite often, God would show up late at night in his seminars, and a sweet anointing would sweep in. He would usually say he felt the power of God in his hands and then begin to gently weep. He would call for a prayer line, and a gentle wave of intense anointing would flow through the room.

I watched, took notes, and became intrigued by how he navigated the supernatural. This is one of the things that I think is imperative when God gives you a front row seat with a general. Stay in student mode. Keep your heart in a posture to learn and grow.

"Be ye followers of me, even as I also am of Christ." (KJV)

Generals can serve as examples to us. They have charted a bold pathway, and there are lessons to be learned, mantles to be caught, and impartation to receive. Some of the greatest lessons are not learned in a classroom but by intentionally observing the function and flow of the leader. I learned so many things about the ways of the Holy Spirit by watching Dr. Hayes and his friends. My flow and call are extremely different than his, but God used him in a significant way in my life to teach me about the anointing and the flow of the Spirit. At first, I learned by observation, but later I would grow by proximity.

I settled into the pace of Bible college and had a phenomenal journey during my time as a student, but graduation was rapidly approaching. It seemed like so many of my fellow students had great ministry job offers, and I was still waiting on mine. I pursued the Lord about this and the desire I now had for full-time ministry. He just kept reassuring my heart, and then suddenly, an offer came. A friendly out-of-state pastor offered me a home, car, and salary if I would go to work for him upon graduating. My prayers had been answered, but there was a glitch! God told me "NO." He told me He wanted me to serve the ministry of Dr. Norvel Hayes. I turned down the job and made the decision to stay even though I had not been offered any kind of ministry job. But I knew I had heard from God.

Let me pause and interject a vital point. Most Elijah/Elisha relationships will have these consequential moments of surrender. In fact, part of God's purpose in the connection is bringing all parties involved to a deeper place of obedience and intergenerational connection.

Right before graduation, a shocking opportunity popped up. The administrator of the Bible college left unexpectedly, and they needed someone to fill the slot. God spoke to Dr. Hayes' daughter Zona, and she asked me to fill in and see if I might be the one. That was the beginning of a much deeper level of connection to the man and ministry of Dr. Norvel Hayes. I went on to serve in that capacity for several years. I even lived with Dr. Hayes for a period of time and was invited into the inner circle of his family. To this day, I consider them extended family. God allowed me to have access to and a close bond with one of the great generals. I preached with him, occasionally traveled with him, and did life with him for many years until he went to be with the Lord. He was the most impactful leader in my life and ministerial development.

I learned a lot from Dr. Hayes in the pulpit, but I probably learned more behind the scenes. For example, I will never forget sitting in a green room (the place where the speakers hang out before and after service) when he shared a story about a minister who had

Dr. Hayes told me that about every ten years or so a new voice launched out in the Body of Christ and took off like a rocket, but sadly, many quickly fell. His life lesson from this observation was that character was a key attribute of ministerial development.

fallen. He told me he had observed that about every ten years or so a new voice launched out in the Body of Christ and took off like a rocket, but sadly, many quickly fell. His life lesson from this observation was that character was a key attribute of ministerial development. In fact, in his many relationships with other generals such as R.W. Schambach and Kenneth E. Hagin, I observed a pattern. They all held personal integrity in high regard and brought discipline to those under them who were not living in accordance to God's Word.

Dr. Hayes also emphasized the importance of training believers to stand on the Word and believe God. He would frequently hold weeklong seminars with worship, teaching, and prayer. The Holy Spirit would come in powerfully, healing and delivering people. He dedicated a lot of time to lay hands on and minister to the people who came from all over. I saw a very interesting pattern. If he focused a lot on praying for people in several services, he would then take a service to just teach and train. He ended with a prayer or worship altar call, but he didn't lay hands on them. I asked him about this, and he told me it was intentional. He wanted the people to learn how to declare the Word, pray, worship God, and get the victory for themselves.

Dr. Hayes believed strongly in casting out devils, but he used an amazingly simple process of prayer and authority. He was not at all formulaic or complicated in his approach. He had learned how to cast out demons early on from Lester Sumrall. When I worked for Dr. Hayes, he would host demonology seminars to teach on deliverance and minister to people who were bound. Those meetings always had such wild things happening! I remember the time that I laid hands on a man, and his eyes transformed in front of me to look like snake eyes. Another time while we were praying, demons were moving around inside of a woman's belly, and we could feel them with our hands. The supernatural was evident during deliverances. We were not allowed to work for Dr. Hayes without being able to minister deliverance to people. He expected every one of his staff members to have faith and authority to cast out demons. It was non-negotiable.

One of the simplest yet most remarkable times I had with Dr. Hayes was after a seminar when an international student brought his father into the back room for prayer. His father needed a miracle in his heart. Dr. Hayes asked me to agree with him. As we prepared to pray, he quoted the Word: "Again I say unto you, that if two of you shall agree on earth as touching any thing that they shall ask, it shall be done for them of my Father which is in Heaven."

My relationship with Dr. Hayes lasted from my teens into my forties when he went home to be with the Lord in his nineties. He was a strong, humble, and faith-filled spiritual father who catapulted me into new levels of faith and authority. It was my joy to serve and be a part of his life and ministry. He was strong-willed and could be extremely inflexible when he was passionate about something. Other times he had the gentlest nature, particularly when he was moving in healing or teaching. When it came to deliverance, he displayed unwavering faith and authority to cast the devil out. He did deliverance in a way that made everyone feel like they could do it.

However, our relationship did not come without tests. One time he rebuked me from the pulpit during a large camp meeting because I was talking with a staff member. The correction was lengthy, and he used it as a teaching moment! It seems funny now, but at the time I was furious. The Lord quickly reminded me of my posture and the value of the relationship, so I adjusted my attitude. One time, during a challenging season, the Lord spoke very strongly to me. He asked me who had initiated the relationship—me or Him (the Lord). I immediately responded that He had initiated it. Then He told me if I was to obey Him, I couldn't release myself. Over time, I realized it was the will of God for me to remain planted with Dr. Hayes until the end. I did that to the best of my ability, and I received rich deposits throughout our long relationship.

Dr. Hayes communicated to me and those I led how much he valued me. I was thankful for his words of affirmation and the fact that he believed in me and saw something in me before many others did. His daughter Zona also had a huge impact on my life, taking me into her family and blessing me in so many ways. After Dr. Hayes passed, several people who knew him well shared conversations that he had with them about me and how proud he was of me. Our bond was strong and our journey long. I had a front row seat in the life of a general, and I learned so many lessons that they could fill volumes. I would do it all over again in a minute!

Chapter Six

MY STORY

Barbara Yoder

Founder/Apostle
Shekinah Regional Apostolic Center
Ann Arbor, Michigan

was busily writing, pouring out my heart and thoughts on paper, when suddenly I realized I had misinterpreted the objective. Though I had almost completed writing about Elijah/Elisha, my work was aimed at a totally different objective. Needless to say, I was upset. I was aware I had wasted all that time producing something that missed the target.

Immersed in frustration and feeling trapped by a deadline, I started re-writing the entire work. It was then that concepts began to pop into my mind, reframing the entire chapter. It jolted me because some of the thoughts about Elijah/Elisha are not ones that are celebrated and focused on today. Yet I had been praying, asking God for both key thoughts and words that released truth and anointing. So I grabbed them! Correct focus and right alignment release Heaven's help on our behalf. This is exactly what happened to Elisha. He realigned to Heaven's plumbline through his encounter with Elijah.

Recently, I read that we know nothing about Elijah until he appeared on the scene. I had never considered that; we don't know what led up to his appearance beginning in 1 Kings 17. Yet he leapt on the scene as a prophet and miracle worker. When was he called as a prophet? Who was involved? What took place? Where did it take place? We have no clue. What we do know is that he was a nation-changing prophet and an astounding miracle worker. We know from 1 Kings 17 that he had power over nature. He was miraculously kept alive both by a raven and a widow. His name meant "Jehovah is my God."

He lived during the reign of King Ahab, whose wife was Jezebel. God called and empowered Elijah to confront a very corrupt governmental system and its leaders, King Ahab and Jezebel. He also led a school of the prophets. These nuggets and the miracles that happened are one side of the importance of Elijah's significance. The other was his relationship with Elisha.

SEED OF DESTINY

What about Elijah and Elisha? God issued an invitation to Elisha to inherit Elijah's mantle—the mantle of governmental authority and miracles. It was a double portion mantle. It required an unusual level of faith encompassed by risk. Furthermore, that mantle required total surrender and submission in order to fulfill the mandate contained within it. Mantles are powerful. They are not to be minimized or treated as common. Elijahs possess mantles to impart to the upcoming generation. They are holy, germinating

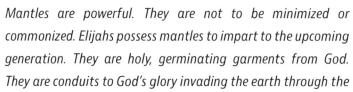

Mantles are powerful. They are not to be minimized or commonized. Elijahs possess mantles to impart to the upcoming generation. They are holy, germinating garments from God. They are conduits to God's glory invading the earth through the human beings possessing them.

garments from God. They are conduits to God's glory invading the earth through the human beings possessing them.

How did that happen? It wasn't because of some easy, emotionally driven relationship. Sometimes I believe we romanticize things based on culturally developed expectations and interpretations by our culture and Western Christianity. Neither did it arise from favoritism or because Elijah really liked Elisha and was enamored of his personality, gifting, and charisma. No, not at all. Out of the clear blue, he went up to Elisha and threw a mantle on him—his mantle. In reality, it was God's mantle!

In fact, when Elijah threw his mantle on Elisha, it was at the lowest and most lonely time in Elijah's life. He was depressed; he thought he was the only one left who stood for righteousness. He had just encountered the prophets of Baal in 1 Kings 18, and he had slayed them all. He felt like God and His angel armies had forsaken him (1Kings 19:14). He was running for his life as a result, running from Jezebel. In the midst of this crisis, God spoke to him among other things to go and anoint Elisha to succeed him. Elijah responded to the word/direction of the Lord, not emotional hype.

The Elijah/Elisha relationship commenced by Elijah throwing his mantle upon Elisha out of the clear blue, with no forewarning or indicators. Bam, there it was—the mantle so large, burying Elisha. In modern terminology I could say he received a prophetic word or sign. That act released a seed of destiny. However, that seed was not according to the will of man but rather the will of God. Elijah did what God told him to do, and that marked Elisha for life. It not only impacted him deeply spiritually, it activated motion, movement, and an immediate response in Elisha. In one explosive moment, Elisha's life was changed forever.

True, significant prophetic words mark someone for destiny. They cannot shake the words; they remember them whether they're following God or running from God. True prophetic words are powerful. They chase down the person until that person either yields or wholeheartedly rebels. True Elijahs wait on the word of the Lord, and when the word comes, they release it, transforming someone's life forever—marking them for destiny with seeds of destiny.

Currently, a very remarkable young man is in relationship with me based on the prophetic word I gave him when I dedicated him as a baby. That word has chased him down—chased him through rebellion, millions of dollars gained and lost, worldly success, everything that people believe life really should be about. Two years ago he contacted me, and since that time, he has stuck to me like glue.

True Elijahs wait on the word of the Lord, and when the word comes, they release it, transforming someone's life forever. Marking them for destiny.

He can't get the word out of his mind, and it is transforming him as well as the whole trajectory of his life. He keeps coming back again and again so I can give him counsel and speak into his life to help him make the important shifts, all because a mantle was thrown on him. He is pursuing me, the gift of God I carry.

Elishas pursue their Elijah. Elijah did not pursue Elisha other than throwing the mantle on him. To have an authentic Elijah/Elisha relationship, it must originate in Heaven. When that occurs, both parties know that relationship is ordained by God and will commit to it regardless of the cost. For Elisha to persevere through everything to apprehend the mantle, he had to know it was God-birthed. Furthermore, it was not the ministry that was released; it was the seed. Elisha first had to submit to the process in order to inherit the mantle.

I've released many seeds of destiny. How many have created the impact Elijah's seed did? I have no clue. However, there is nothing more fulfilling than to know someone has received that seed, not into their emotions but into their spirit, and activated it. It both marks them as well as marks their relationship with me, their Elijah.

The second part of that process shifts from Elijah to Elisha. Will the Elisha fully take the seed of destiny into his spirit as the original Elisha did? Will he make an immediate course correction? Elijah released the seed, the impartation—but would Elisha activate it and position himself for germination?

This positioning was not a simple thing, it would require of Elisha a total surrender of his life as he had known it. And he had much to give up. Because of the description given of what he had to burn (tear down, release any connections to his natural life) it would require a complete release of both who he had been (identity) and what he possessed (riches). He faced the same dilemma the rich young ruler did.

In 1 Kings 19:21, *The Message Bible* says that Elisha took his yoke of oxen and butchered them. He made a fire with his plow and tackle, then boiled the meat and threw a farewell meal for his family. Then he left and followed Elijah, becoming his right hand man.

Elisha first honored his past, his family, and his previous blessings by throwing a dinner for them. In that act was both honor for those who brought him this far as well as clarity in separation. He loved his family and all the people and things associated with it. He had a heart of gratitude. But it was also an official pronouncement of separation from them as his primary life source to now join Elijah, who represented God.

One of the most disheartening things I have experienced is to see the anointed power of the word, the seed of destiny, released to somebody who chooses to go the wrong way. I've watched several receive and be impacted by the prophetic seed of destiny, yet return to what is comfortable to them. Once God releases His word—that seed of destiny—He is serious. To ignore this is to reject God in an act of rebellion, saying, "My way is better, easier, less perilous, more certain, or whatever, than God's word."

IMPACT FOR TRANSFORMATION

Elijah's word had great impact, changing the trajectory of Elisha's life. Furthermore, Elisha chose (whether he was immediately aware of it or not) to be demoted rather than promoted. I've realized over the years that several people who decided to follow me were not willing to be demoted. They thought their association with me would build their platform, notoriety, or whatever. It's not a great feeling to wake up one morning and realize it was not really me they wanted, but where I could get them. I awakened to the reality of being used. And by the way, it was also an opportunity for me to learn to take the highroad.

I have never stopped immensely valuing, honoring, admiring, and loving the leader who imparted the initial seed of destiny in my life. Though it was not an up close and personal relationship, it was one of life-changing impact and impartation. It marked me; changed my life forever. That relationship injected me with a seed of destiny. Though that leader did not recognize the impact she made on me, I have never forgotten it. And through prophetic words, others have recognized and highlighted that relationship. I was told prophetically several times that I had this leader's mantle. I say that to stress the fact that it's not always a personal, up close relationship.

One of the things that unsettles my spirit is the frequent conversation among the emerging generation concerning finding those key people who can help build their platform. Elisha wasn't looking for Elijah to build his platform. He gave his life to God by giving it to Elijah. He paid the price for the mantle. His eyes were totally on God!

―――――― ⟨⟨⟩⟩ ――――――

God's authentic call and ministry are birthed in humility, surrender, abandoned love for God, and people. Jesus said that except you deny yourself, take up your cross and follow Him, you won't find life (Matthew 16:24). The power in ministry is found in those that have made that decision.

―――――― ⟨⟨⟩⟩ ――――――

God's authentic call and ministry are birthed in humility and surrender, as well as an abandoned love for God and people. Jesus said that except you deny yourself, take up your cross and follow Him, you won't find life (Matthew 16:24). The power in ministry is found in those that have made that decision. To die is to live, to lose is to gain! God's Kingdom is an upside down Kingdom. Promotion doesn't come from the east, west, north, or south; it comes from the Lord. God puts down one, and He sets up another (Psalms 75:6–7).

However, the heart of a true mentor—Elijah—wants to create space for budding ministries to have experience and be seen. I've given developing ministries which are unseen, unnoticed, and unrecognized an opportunity to speak and minister. Even then, though I've made room for them, it's their gift that creates new spheres and levels of ministry. The Word of God says your gift will make room for you; it will open doors for you (Proverbs 18:16).

Elijah Wasn't Warm and Fuzzy

There are several images of Elijah projected in the Bible. The spirit of Elijah was proclaimed to be a restorative anointing. In Malachi, it says the spirit of Elijah would appear on the scene before the great and terrible day of the Lord, turning the hearts of the fathers to the children and the hearts of the children to the fathers to prevent a curse from being released (Malachi 4:5-6). That means there has to be a fathering anointing resting upon any Elijah leader. But that isn't necessarily a warm and fuzzy feeling or relationship. Fathers call us to attention!

Elisha's responsibility, which lasted until the day Elijah was taken up into Heaven, was to serve him, help him, be subservient to him, and pour water on his hands (2 Kings 3:11). It looked totally menial. What people don't realize is that something supernatural was happening. Elisha was catching Elijah's spirit. That's not exactly a ministry most would stand in line to sign up for. They are looking for flashing lights, sirens, billboards, TV appearances, goosebumps, etc. Yet underground, without any fanfare, something far more powerful than fame or fortune was forming Elisha into a vessel that could receive Elijah's mantle.

Billye Brim for 10 years hid behind a desk, transcribing and committing to print all of Kenneth Hagin's teachings. What if she had thought she was above that? What if she had thought of it as just menial work? It was 10 years of hard work. Simultaneously, God was planting within her a treasury of wisdom and knowledge as well as a transference of anointing that would later bring her into prominence and her unique God identity. However, she was not seeking prominence; she was seeking faithfulness to a holy God!

It's not always easy to give your life away to someone greater than you. The end result is worth it, but sometimes, even often, that position requires constant attitude adjustment. I remember the sense of destiny I had sitting under this amazing ministry. Because of the leader's age and the size of the congregation, she had no time for me personally. However, there was something inside of me that would not let go, and I got as close as I could to her, taking as much as I could and absorbing everything she had from afar.

From what I can gather, Elijah didn't sit around affirming Elisha. He went about his prophet duties. Elisha had to follow him, pursue him. Today, so many quickly get offended and leave because they're not constantly being affirmed, built up, encouraged, told what to do and how to do it, spending hours and hours with the one they think they want to be like. Elisha caught the mantle by observation and association, not a case of the fuzzy-wuzzies. I know a prominent leader who told me how the mantle of a particular historic figure came on him by reading this person's book. Don't let your expectations hijack your call!

Elijah even tempted Elisha to leave him. He kept saying, "I'm going here, but you don't have to go." It was up to Elisha to remember that the mantle had been thrown on him and to follow Elijah regardless of what Elijah said. Elisha's response to Elijah's constant discouragement to follow him was to become even more persistent. Basically, he said, "I'm going to see you taken up into Heaven because God has destined that I wear the mantle you've worn. I will not give up prematurely, come hell or high water. I will persevere to the end to inherit what God has destined for me." Elisha not only apprehended the mantle but a double portion of it. An interesting fact is that He never did reach the level of fame that Elijah did. However, he was powerful in his own right because he wore Elijah's mantle.

Matthew 11:11-14 says there is a company of prophets coming in the spirit of Elijah. Furthermore, it links Elijah with that breakthrough, overcoming, non-compromising, incomparable force of God's Spirit and Kingdom. That same section of Matthew 11 says that the Kingdom of Heaven suffers violence, and the violent take it by force. This end-time company of prophets arising is an invincible spiritual force in the earth, apprehending the kingdoms of this world for God's Kingdom. God said it's not by force, it's not by might or power, but it's by His Spirit (Zechariah 4:6).

I believe that in this hour God is looking for both real Elijahs and Elishas. Elijah was a real prophet, not one looking for fame, money, position, tokens of wealth, notoriety, etc. He was intent on fulfilling the will of God. He was sold out. He was not tainted by either the prevailing culture or other leaders.

We live in an age in which Hollywood has hijacked our image of success. I've been disturbed over and over because of the current mentality prevalent among both generations seeking tokens of success. I believe that God wants us to prosper. But what we could do with the money that is often spent frivolously for a look—a look that says, "I am successful."

Elijah was not just a restorer of the generations, but a forerunning spirit that called a generation to repentance. John the Baptist came in the spirit of Elijah, crying out, "Repent, for the kingdom of Heaven is at hand." His mission was to prepare the way for the people to receive Jesus. Those who were baptized in John's baptism saw Jesus for who He was when He came on the scene.

That spirit of Elijah ultimately has to bow to the King of Kings and the Lord of Lords, just as Elisha bowed low before Elisha. It was even hard for John the Baptist (who came in the spirit of Elijah and was the greatest prophet known to man) to bow to one greater. When Jesus appeared on the scene and John ended up in prison, John began to doubt that Jesus was the Lamb of God who came to take away the sin of the world. He faltered.

Neither Elijah nor Elisha was perfect. They struggled with carnality when push came to shove. But they ended up triumphant. Elijah stayed true to who he was, and Elisha persevered to the end. A company is arising in the spirit of Elijah that will apprehend the kingdoms of this world for God. 1 Corinthians 15:24 says Jesus will deliver them to GOD. How is Jesus going to apprehend them? Through us! And we are the ones who will deliver them to Jesus.

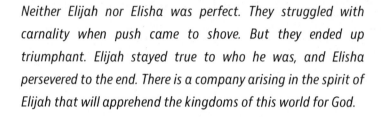

Neither Elijah nor Elisha was perfect. They struggled with carnality when push came to shove. But they ended up triumphant. Elijah stayed true to who he was, and Elisha persevered to the end. There is a company arising in the spirit of Elijah that will apprehend the kingdoms of this world for God.

This truth infuses me with faith because we are in the time when both the Elijahs and Elishas are going to arise and connect in powerful ways that change the face of the earth and governments, releasing double portions, the miraculous beyond anything we've known—a generation older and younger coming together, loving not their lives unto death and risking all for God's Kingdom to be established on earth. Let it be so.

Chapter Seven

WHEN GENERATIONS RUN TOGETHER

Joshua Giles

Senior Pastor/Prophet
Kingdom Embassy Church
Minneapolis, Minnesota

I grew up in a Christian household that jumpstarted my journey into learning the qualities of serving. My parents were both pastors, and I learned early on the challenges and the rewards of ministry. First, the challenges of ministry made me want to run from any form of serving publicly within the church. I watched my pastors endure tests of betrayal, extreme warfare, and financial hardship, all for the sake of a cause that they were willing to suffer for. It would be some years later before I would even begin to understand the true value of faith in Jesus Christ. As I developed a deep, personal relationship with the Lord, I grew to understand that suffering for something or someone you love is actually an honor. That was the moment my eyes opened up to the beautiful reward of serving in ministry. I looked beyond the challenges to see the countless lives that had been impacted by the message of the Gospel—the reward of seeing broken people healed, rejected people accepted into the family of Christ, and the lost found, receiving their God-given identity. The reward of serving is priceless. The quality of serving is the key to being fulfilled in life.

Years later, I found myself engulfed in the study of Elijah and Elisha. This spiritual father and son relationship intrigued me. It models a deep, dynamic relationship in which two generations merge together to fulfill an assignment given by God in the earth. This is powerful! These kinds of relationships are even more important now because of the assault of the enemy against families, both natural and spiritual children and parents. The enemy has waged warfare against multi-generations coming together because he knows there is power and impact in those alignments. I believe God is releasing the spirit of Elijah to restore fractured families and heal a rift in the Body of Christ between generations. We will truly see the hearts of fathers turn toward the sons and the hearts of sons turn toward the fathers.

Over a decade ago, I found myself in one of the most vulnerable and broken places of my life. I was traveling around the country preaching and ministering to others, but my life and the world as I knew it was falling apart. Someone I had looked up to in ministry for years had spiraled down into a destructive pattern due to unhealed soul wounds. Ministries were displaced, relationships broken, and people were hurting. A myriad of questions raced through my mind: *How could this have happened? Why won't this person humble himself and get help? Where does this leave me?* I went into a period of consecration, fasting, and prayer.

After several months, the Lord spoke to me and said, "I had to allow your world to fall apart because I'm bringing you into a new world." I thought, What does this mean? God said to me, "The spiritual place that you have been in is not conducive to where I'm taking you. I'm sending you a father who will pour into you, correct you, and prepare you for your purpose." It was when I was most broken, that my spiritual father—my Elijah— entered into my life. And the journey began.

FINDING IDENTITY

As an Elisha, the greatest lesson I have learned is that I did not know who I was. I thought I knew who I was, but I had no clue. I had taken on fragments of who people wanted me to be and what I thought people would like. I hid behind a cloak disguised as my personality. Negative bloodline issues emerge when you are not walking in your identity in Christ. In biology, this is known as epigenetics: "The study of the chemical modification of specific genes or gene-associated proteins of an organism. Epigenetic modifications can define how the information in genes is expressed and used by cells." [5]

In other words, epigenetics is a pattern or gene sequence that is placed on top of one's DNA ("epi" means "on top of"). Studies have shown that what a person's ancestors have experienced is hidden within the DNA of generations after them. For instance, if a group of people has gone through trauma, it can manifest in a descendant's DNA, without them ever having experienced the same trauma. Experts have compared these markers in the DNA to flipping on a switch. Epigenetics studies show that the wrong environment can bring out these triggers or markers within the blood. For example, an unstable environment can trigger a mental disorder that was lying dormant, or a fear-filled environment could trigger an autoimmune disease.

---

5 https://www.britannica.com/science/epigenetics

A study conducted in 2015 by Rachel Yehuda and her team at the Icahn School of Medicine at Mount Sinai in New York published results from observing descendants of Holocaust survivors who were either interned in Nazi concentrations camps or forced into hiding during World War II.[6] These survivors were exposed to torture and immense trauma. After it was over, they went on to live their lives. But the study focused on their descendants. Although their descendants were not exposed to torture or trauma, there were invisible markers that altered a gene linked to their levels of cortisol. The results are controversial and disputed by some; however, the study found that the offspring of those Holocaust survivors were predisposed to anxiety disorders.

Our understanding from a natural, scientific perspective also relates to the spiritual. Experiences, as well as deeds done by previous generations, can pass down a bloodline. Deuteronomy 5:9 explains that the iniquity of the fathers can manifest itself up to the third and fourth generations.

The good news is that Jesus Christ broke the curse, blotted out the iniquity, destroyed the yoke, and severed the bondage of the enemy. But it is only through receiving the spirit of adoption that we fully experience this freedom (see Romans 8:15). The Lord has raised up fathers and mothers in the faith to point the way to freedom. They have the ability to change the spiritual gene sequence in order to push sons and daughters into divine purpose. They are called to nurture, correct, and instruct us so that we can become more like Christ. Through biblical spiritual fathering, bloodline

---

6 https://www.bbc.com/future/article/20190326-what-is-epigenetics#:~:text=A%202015%20study%20found%20that,involved%20in%20the%20stress%20response.

The Lord has raised up fathers and mothers in the faith to point the way to freedom. They have the ability to change the spiritual gene sequence in order to push sons and daughters into divine purpose. They are called to nurture, correct, and instruct us so that we can become more like Christ.

curses are broken, and we receive the identity of the Heavenly Father. The word "father" in the New Testament is the Greek word "pater." It is where we get the English word "pattern" from. Spiritual fathers and mothers are patterns. They chart paths, take spiritual hits, and pioneer so that we can walk through unhindered. The apostle Paul often spoke of his assignment as a spiritual father. He described his experience as birthing those that were accountable to his ministry until Christ was formed in them:

"My little children, for whom I am again in the anguish of childbirth until Christ is formed in you." (Galatians 4:19 ESV)

As an Elisha, I have learned the need for spiritual parenting on this level. In Scripture, God used Elijah to imprint his anointing and will on the heart and life of Elisha. God superimposed His DNA through fathering into the life of Elisha. Likewise, God used my spiritual father to lead me to rediscover my true identity in Christ. He has pointed me to Christ, taught me biblical principles, and shown me the need for accountability. I have had the privilege of traveling and ministering with him in conferences and church services. Identity is truly found in the coming together of the generations. When the hearts of fathers and sons unite, we will carry a deeper depth of the image of Christ.

THE NEED FOR ACCOUNTABILITY

One of the most memorable phrases that my spiritual father spoke to me was, "The greater the gift, the greater the need for accountability." Being accountable is submitting one's actions and decisions to be inspected or properly judged by someone else. Accountability is a safeguard—a protective measure for the one who chooses it. There are several benefits of an Elisha being accountable to Elijah:

Accountability develops character.

Accountability provides a hedge of protection.

Accountability unlocks wisdom.

Accountability brings clarity and eradicates confusion.

Accountability fosters growth.

Accountability positions you to receive impartation.

Accountability releases God's favor upon your life.

Being accountable to a spiritual leader requires submission. Unfortunately, we belong to a generation that has been abused, mishandled, and even spiritually assaulted under the guise of submission. The enemy has fueled this twisting of spiritual authority in order to cause people to back away from pure and true submission to proper spiritual authority. I believe that in the coming days, we will see a wave of inner healing come to a generation that has been rejected, abandoned, and mistreated. The Lord is raising up those who truly have His heart to pour into others. Submission is a beautiful thing when done the biblical way. Submission means, "the action or fact of accepting or yielding to a superior force or to the will or authority of another person."[7]

---

7 Definition from Oxford Languages

Submission is an act of the will. When Jesus was in the Garden of Gethsemane, He was teaching us submission to the Father. Although in the flesh He wanted the bitter cup to pass from Him, He knew it was the will of the Father that He drink of that cup. He spoke those famous words, "Not my will, but yours be done" (Luke 22:42).

As spiritual sons and daughters, we must learn that we are here to carry out the will of the Father. He has ordained spiritual authority, but we must freely and willingly submit to it. Spiritual authority is the compass that will help to guide us during tough times. It is a beacon of light in the darkness.

POSITIONED FOR IMPARTATION

My spiritual father was in Houston, teaching and ministering at a service under a heavy anointing. I flew in from Minneapolis just for this event. The Lord had placed it upon my heart that there was an impartation for me. Several people I knew were at the service. They pastored churches in various cities. As the service ended, I was standing in the sanctuary with a group of people, talking and laughing. I had really been enjoying the fellowship and the word that came forth. Immediately, he walked up to me in front of all of these people and proceeded to ask me a list of questions. He had a very authoritative tone and his questions seemed personal. He started by saying, "I need an account of what's going on in your life and ministry. If I am your spiritual father, then I have the right to ask concerning your character, actions, and decisions." Standing there in front of other pastors and leaders, I had to give an open account of personal, ministry, and other details. Then he abruptly said, "I need to see you after the next service."

Honestly, I was embarrassed. It seemed as though I was in trouble and had done something wrong. I sat through the next service, nervous about what the meeting might entail. But I pressed through to worship and receive the word. After the service, I tracked him down privately. He then began to correct me in some areas of my personal life. I humbled myself to receive because I knew this was the Lord. The undertone of his voice was infused with love. Although the things he was saying were stern, the love of Christ was there. He said to me, "The Lord said to me I need to spend more time pouring into you. Every Tuesday we will talk. I will share the word with you and impart to you."

This started a journey of impartation through the teaching of the Word. Those Tuesday sessions went on for some years. Although I was pastoring a growing church and ministering around the country and abroad, I had a pastor who was teaching me each week. Now the times and days have changed, but I still receive teaching and impartation from him. I value those times of impartation even more now. The words that he has personally shared with me have healed brokenness in my soul, built my faith, empowered me to step out on the instructions that God had given me, and helped me to avoid pitfalls. Through this experience, I learned that you must be positioned to receive impartation. It is not about a natural positioning, but a posture of the heart. Further, I learned the necessity of being poured into. I had gone for years pouring into others and had not consistently been poured into. I could feel my spirit being strengthened. I was being equipped for the work of the ministry. Even more importantly than that, my soul was being cared for and pastored.

I find that some only want the gift a person has. They want the performance, the skill, or the talent of an individual, but they do not care about the soul of that person. True Elijahs place the person before their gift. Our character and who we are is more important than how well we can perform. It is only when placing the person ahead of their gift that you come to realize people are the real gifts. Walking alongside my spiritual father has shown me that God loved me enough to send me help. He loves me so much that He desires to instruct and teach me. He loves me so much that He corrects my heart in love.

In addition, an Elijah carries a depth of wisdom that Elisha needs. Throughout my journey, I have found that wisdom is essential. You cannot rely on your talent to navigate the difficulties of life and ministry. It requires experience, wisdom, and knowledge. As the Lord is merging the generations, a fusion of wisdom and strength is taking place. Job 2:12 says, "Wisdom is found with the elderly, and understanding comes with long life." We need the wisdom of the older generation. They know the path we should take. Furthermore, 1 John 2:14 says, "I write to you, young men, because you are strong." The young generation has a strength and stamina that only comes with youth. When the two generations come together and combine strength and wisdom, we are unstoppable against the plans and plots of the devil. Our Christian faith is generational. The blessing of God is generational. Our God is a God of generations! With that being said, I am excited to be an Elisha running with the Elijah God has assigned me to.

When the two generations come together and combine strength and wisdom, we are unstoppable against the plans and plots of the devil. Our Christian faith is generational.

Chapter Eight

FROM FATHER TO SON

Sherman Dumas

Apostle
All Nations Worship Assembly San Bernardino
San Bernardino, California

We see throughout Scriptures how important spiritual fatherhood and sonship are in the Kingdom. Elisha, for example, understood that his next level was locked inside Elijah. Likewise, I recognize that my next level is locked inside my spiritual father. Fathers see beyond the sons' ability to see. For a son to benefit from this insight, he must flow in submission and trust toward his (or her) father.

The prophet Isaiah gives us a picture of what occurs when spiritual fathers are not in place and instead, the people are subject to the leadership of babes. Isaiah 3:4 states, "I will give children to be their princes, and babes shall rule over them." The subsequent verses in Isaiah 3 unfold the consequences:

- The people become oppressed by one another other (v. 5)
- The child will be insolent toward the elder (v. 5)

- The base will be insolent toward the honorable (v. 5)
- An immense lack of identity will be evident (v. 6)

SONS TO A FATHER

To fully understand spiritual fatherhood and sonship in the Kingdom, we first need to understand the grace and relationship dynamic of our own adoption as sons (see Romans 15:17). Many believers, including anointed ministers, have not been able to fully understand and live out this relationship. They know *in theory* they are sons but do not think and relate to God that way in practice. Like the prodigal son in Jesus' parable, they are forever coming to God hoping to be treated as one of the servants. The prodigal said to himself, "I will … go back to my father and say … 'I am no longer worthy to be called your son; make me like one of your hired men'"(Luke 15:18-19). Most Christians relate to God as a disciple to a teacher, or a servant to a master, rather than as a son to a father.

Of course, we are all disciples and servants, as well as sons. Our problem is that we relate to God out of a servant's mentality, which He never intended. We still subconsciously think of ourselves as unworthy to be sons. It is a tremendous breakthrough when we discover the true nature of grace and relationship with God and learn to come to Him with the confidence of a first-born son. Then we walk in the grace of God and find it has great power.

Next, God's purpose is that we not only relate to Him as sons to a father, but that we also relate to those over us in the church as sons to a father. Our relationship with those over us in the Lord is not meant to be distant, formal, religious, hierarchical, mechanical, or institutional. Neither is it meant to be untrusting or impersonal. It is meant to be *very* personal. It is meant to be very personal. It should be the trusting, relaxed, intimate, caring, gracious, non-legalistic, warm, selfless, giving, honoring, and committed relationship of a good family, without any private agenda.

In a good family, we care about others and we live for each other. Despite what ups and downs there may be, the most important thing is maintaining healthy, appropriate, personal relationships with one another.

We do not need to submit ourselves to leaders who are tyrants. We have all heard stories of manipulative, controlling leaders and problems caused by deceptive and inappropriate religious leaders. We are free to obey Christ and not men when they have a wrong spirit or personal agenda, just as the apostles told us, "We must obey God rather than men!" (Acts 5:29). These words, however, must never be used with an arrogant independence, contrary to the spirit of the Word of God that calls us into community. Paul made it clear that God uses leadership authority to bring about obedience to God:

> "I will not venture to speak of anything except what Christ has accomplished through me in leading the Gentiles to obey God by what I have said and done." (Romans 15:18 NIV)

We are, however, to give allegiance from the heart to true apostolic fathers. Such fathers are not controlling or motivated by greed or personal ambition but have the heart of God to care for us and all the saints. Here, from the heart of the apostle John, is an example of fatherly care:

> "I have no greater joy than to hear that my children are walking in the truth." (3 John 4 NIV)

Here is one from Paul:

"My dear children, for whom I am again in the pains of childbirth until Christ is formed in you, how I wish I could be with you now and change my tone, because I am perplexed about you!" (Galatians 4:19-20 NIV).

Spiritual fathers love their sons, and spiritual sons serve and honor their fathers. The relationship is mutually beneficial and involves mutual giving. The son gives, and the father gives. They honor one another, and each wants the other to succeed. These are life-giving and freedom-giving relationships, for an apostle loves to see other people set free. There is accountability and authority, but not control—a true father does not create dependency. Like a dad with his family, the way in which fatherly authority is exercised varies greatly depending on the maturity of the son. As sons become more mature, they also become more independent, yet all the while remain strongly bonded in love to their spiritual father. *These values are central to the ministry of Jesus Christ.*

Jesus Himself is our example:

Therefore, holy brothers, who share in the heavenly calling, fix your thoughts on Jesus, the apostle and high priest whom we confess. He was faithful to the one who appointed him, just as Moses was faithful in all God's house. (Hebrews 3:1-3)

Notice a fascinating phrase here, which is definitive of both the relationships and the nature of the apostolic church. Following the instruction to focus our full attention upon Him, it states that Christ, as an apostle, was *"faithful to the one who appointed him."* This piece of information is of the utmost importance.

Holiness and obedience to God are defined as much by your fellowship with, attitude to, and treatment of others, as it is by what goes on in your heart and mind or your service to Christ.

We also see in the New Testament that Christ and the apostles spent as much time instructing us on how to love and relate to others as they did on how to respond to God and pursue Christ. Holiness and obedience to God are defined as much by our fellowship with, attitude to, and treatment of others, as by what goes on in our heart and mind or our service to Christ.

Much could be said concerning this, but ultimately, I desire to make one point. Each of us is meant to find the "spirit of sonship" in our relationships in the church as well as in our relationship with God. If we miss this, we will miss the way and the purposes of God. But when we relate to those over us in the Lord as sons to a father, we will have effectively discovered and entered into the real life God intended for the body of Christ. This is church reformation, and it will result in community transformation.

The Key of Honor

"A son honors his father, and a servant his master. If I am a father, where is the honor due me?" (Malachi 1:6)

Sons must posture themselves to honor their fathers. The giving of honor is a key principle if we desire a better life. Not only do the Scriptures call us to honor God (1 Timothy 1:17), we are also called to honor every person in authority over us (Romans 13:7, 1 Peter 2:17). This is especially true of our parents and the leaders of the church.

The command to honor our father and mother was the only commandment that had a promise attached to it—and it is a very specific kind of promise.

> Honor your father and your mother, as the LORD your God has commanded you, so that you may live long and that it may go well with you in the land the LORD your God is giving you." (Deuteronomy 5:16 NIV)

This is the promise of a *longer* life and a *better* life to those who give honor. The New Testament renews the promise which was given under the old covenant (Ephesians 6:1-3) and shows that the giving of honor is a life-giving principle.

The elders who govern the church, in particular those responsible for teaching, are to be especially honored. They are worthy of double honor, says Paul.

> "The elders who direct the affairs of the church well are worthy of double honor, especially those whose work is preaching and teaching." (1 Timothy 5:17 NIV)

When sons fail to honor their father, they fail to walk in the fullness of the blessing of God. If sons do not honor their fathers, the promises and great blessings that attach themselves to the giving of honor are not appropriated.

In the church, which is established by the power of Christ through relationships, the giving of honor is central to Christ's purpose. If we lack in the giving of honor, we lack grace. When our hearts are pure, so that we love to give honor, we are Christlike.

FROM FATHER TO SON

Sonship: The Secret to Spiritual Inheritance

Sonship is the secret to spiritual inheritance. Wherever the Bible speaks of sonship, we discover that in close proximity it speaks of inheritance also. For example:

> But when the time had fully come, God sent his Son, born of a woman, born under law, to redeem those under law, that we might receive the full rights of sons. Because you are sons, God sent the Spirit of his Son into our hearts, the Spirit who calls out, "Abba, Father." So you are no longer a slave, but a son; and since you are a son, God has made you also an heir. (Galatians 4:4-7 NIV).

The Bible makes extensive reference to our inheritance, and there are two stages in receiving inheritance. Ultimately, we obtain the amazing provisions of God, things that really cannot be described (1 Corinthians 2:9), which come to us after the Day of the Lord, which is the day of our redemption.

> Having believed, you were marked in him with a seal, the promised Holy Spirit, who is a deposit guaranteeing our inheritance until the redemption of those who are God's possession…And do not grieve the Holy Spirit of God, with whom you were sealed for the day of redemption. (Ephesians 1:13-14, 4:30-31 NIV)

This vast future inheritance, in which we jointly sharing everything Christ inherits, is preserved for us by the power of God, "…an inheritance that can never perish, spoil or fade—kept in Heaven for you" (1 Peter 1:4-5).

In addition to future inheritance, there is also much we are meant to receive while in our bodies on the earth. We are told to "imitate those who through faith and patience inherit what has been promised" (Hebrews 6:12), and, in the case of Abraham, who in this text is referred to as one we should imitate, it is clear there is also an inheritance for here and now, since "after waiting patiently, Abraham received what was promised" (Hebrews 6:15).

As believers, there are a number of ways that we receive the things we need and which God has promised. We exercise faith to receive answers to prayer; we walk in the principles of sowing and reaping; we believe the promises and receive their outcome as sons would receive an inheritance; and over and above all these, there is abundant and merciful grace.

I want to make a distinction between receiving from God on the basis of sowing and reaping and receiving from God what is promised as inheritance given to sons.

The laws of sowing and reaping are universal, and everyone may benefit by this provision. Many scriptures attest to this, such as 2 Corinthians 9: 6-11 and Luke 6:38. Every believer should participate in sowing and reaping, or giving and receiving as Paul called it in Philippians 4:15. Then we are blessed and benefitted by the laws of harvest. It is God's will that all of us work and believe for a great harvest. God promised He would enlarge the harvest of our righteousness and make us rich in every way so we can always be generous, to the glory of God (see 2 Corinthians 9: 10-11). These laws of harvest are to benefit us and the Kingdom of Christ, both spiritually and materially.

However, the harvest field requires our labor, in the form of good stewardship of our wealth, our regular generosity, and our exercise of faith. We must learn how to sow by faith, and we must also learn how to reap our harvest by faith. Therefore, we work for a harvest.

But inheritance is obtained differently. We do not work for inheritance but simply *receive* it. Inheritance comes because of relationship. We are members of the family, and specifically, first-born sons. Sons do not work for their inheritance, although as a member of the family a good son will certainly work hard for his father. For a son, both the motivation for service and the manner in which reward or provision is received are entirely different from that of an employee.

Consider the following scripture:

> For it is written that Abraham had two sons, one by the slave woman and the other by the free woman. His son by the slave woman was born in the ordinary way; but his son by the free woman was born as the result of a promise. These things may be taken figuratively, for the women represent two covenants. One covenant is from Mount Sinai and bears children who are to be slaves: This is Hagar. Now Hagar stands for Mount Sinai in Arabia and corresponds to the present city of Jerusalem, because she is in slavery with her children. But the Jerusalem that is above is free, and she is our mother. ...But what does the Scripture say? "Get rid of the slave woman and her son, for the slave woman's son will never share in the inheritance with the free woman's son." (Galatians 4:22-26, 30 NIV)

The two sons of Abraham represent people in the church today. There are those that have, albeit unknowingly, a slave mentality, and there are those who live as sons of a promise. We mentioned earlier the tendency for many to continue coming to the Father as the prodigal did, hoping to be treated as one of the servants. The prodigal in Jesus' story was not received as a servant, but as an honored son, yet many in the church, even though God has received them as sons, continue to function as if they were slaves.

A slave, servant, or hired hand does not receive inheritance. Likewise, any Christian with this mentality will find it difficult to receive through *inheritance,* because to receive anything from God requires faith, and faith for inheritance is effectively absent in a slave mentality. Remember there is a spiritual principle that says, *"the slave woman's son will never share in the inheritance with the free woman's son" (Galatians 4:30).* To walk in the abundant provisions of inheritance made by God for His children in this life, one must walk in the freedom of the spirit of sonship. This must be, by faith, our experience of God, not just a theory.

The things that we obtain by inheritance are all those things that are *promised.* Abraham's son by the free woman was born as "the result of a promise," and all sons that walk in the inheritance provisions of God look to the promises so as to receive them. This includes anointing for ministry and the power to do what God has called us to in the Kingdom.

As an aside, I do not wish to imply that *inheritance* replaces *harvest,* or that believing the promises displaces the need for generosity, or for sowing and reaping. Actually, both are needed for us to be complete in faith and righteousness (James 1:4, 2: 22).

Most people assign inheritance to death, meaning a father has to die in order for us receive what is ours. But according to Luke 10:17: "Then the seventy returned with joy, saying, 'Lord, even the demons are subject to us in Your name.'" Jesus was still walking the earth, but his disciples/sons had already begun to receive from Him and operate therein. I am constantly receiving divine impartation from my spiritual father in his writing, in our conversations, and every time I'm present when he is ministering.

THERE IS DIVINE TRANSFER AVAILABLE AND GOD IS RELEASING IT TO THROUGH FATHERS TO SONS.

Elisha is great example of this divine transfer:

> And Elisha saw it, and he cried out, "My father, my father, the chariot of Israel and its horsemen!" So he saw him no more. And he took hold of his own clothes and tore them into two pieces. ¹He also took up the mantle of Elijah that had fallen from him, and went back and stood by the bank of the Jordan. Then he took the mantle of Elijah that had fallen from him, and struck the water, and said, "Where *is* the LORD God of Elijah?" And when he also had struck the water, it was divided this way and that; and Elisha crossed over. (1 Kings 2:12-14)

By way of the divine transfer Elisha received from his father Elijah, he was able to do double what his father saw in his lifetime.

Elijah's 8 miracles:

1. He shuts up the heavens, causing a drought and opening to cause rain.	1 Kings 17:14, 41-46
2. He multiplies flour and oil.	1 Kings 17:7-16
3. He raises the widow's son from the dead.	1 Kings 17:17-24
4. He defeats the prophets of Baal.	1 Kings 18:16-40
5. He is fed by ravens.	1 Kings 17:2-8
6. He destroys Ahaziah's soldiers with lightning.	2 Kings 1:9-13
7. He parts the Jordan River.	2 Kings 2:8
8. He is taken to Heaven in God's chariot.	2 Kings 2:9-18

Elisha's 16 miracles:

1. He parts the Jordan River.	2 Kings 2:14-15
2. He purifies water.	2 Kings 2: 19-22

3. He curses attackers who are then savaged by bears.	2 Kings 2: 23-25
4. He causes a flood to foil the Moabites.	2 Kings 3: 14-25
5. Miraculous flow of oil for the poor widow	2 Kings 4: 2-7
6. Fertility to the woman of Shunem	2 Kings 4: 8-17
7. He raises a child from the dead.	2 Kings 4:32-37
8. He purifies poisoned soup.	2 Kings 4:38-41
9. He multiplies loaves to feed a large crowd.	2 Kings 4:42-44
10. He heals Naaman of leprosy.	2 Kings 5: 1-19
11. Gehazi is cursed with leprosy.	2 Kings 5:20-27
12. He makes an iron axe head float.	2 Kings 6:1-7
13. The Aramaeans are struck with sun blindness, and he then cures them.	2 Kings 6: 15-23
14. He predicts the end of a famine.	2 Kings 7:1-20
15. He prophesies the death of Ben-Hadad and the rise of Hazael.	2 Kings 8:7-15
16. He predicts Israel will defeat Aram three times.	2 Kings 13:14-19

God's answer for the continual advancement of His Kingdom is sonship

All Your works shall praise You, O LORD, and Your saints shall bless You. They shall speak of the glory of Your kingdom, and talk of Your power, to make known to the sons of men His mighty acts, and the glorious majesty of His kingdom. **Your kingdom is an everlasting kingdom, and Your dominion endures throughout all generations. (Psalm 145:10-13 NKJV)**

Chapter Nine

WALKING TOGETHER

Tony Kim

Founder/Pastor
Renaissance International and Roar Collective
Bakersfield, California

A previous move of God has always criticized the next move of God," is a statement I've heard Bill Johnson, Senior Pastor of Bethel Church in Redding, CA, make a number of times. Would this mean, then, that the previous generation withholds their blessing from the following one? If this is the case, it does not reflect God's heart. He gave His promise to Abraham, Isaac, and Jacob (Gen. 50:24). He is the God of generations.

There has been a lot of focus on "passing the baton" from generation to generation, which is what we should do. However, we need to better understand how God works from generation to generation and within the generations. In a relay, four runners run a leg of the race. When one runner comes to the end of his leg of the race, he passes the baton to the next runner to begin the next leg of the race, and so forth. Within the dynamics of the exchange, when the previous runner is releasing the baton to the next runner before he takes off, for a brief moment, both runners are holding the baton at the same time. This is an expression of two generations walking together.

Elijah and Elisha, Moses and Joshua, and Paul and Timothy are a few prime examples of "passing the baton." However, something I often look into is the "principle of first mention," so the first time we see not only the passing of the baton but also two generations working together, building together, and serving one another is with Abraham and Isaac.

Currently, there are three major generations on the earth, while a fourth generation is rising: 1) The Baby Boomers, 2) Generation X, 3) Millennials, and 4) Gen Z. I am a Generation X'er. I propose that the modern-day Abraham Generation today is the Baby Boomers, the Isaac Generation is the Generation X'ers, and the Jacob Generation is the Millennials.

I will briefly touch on the Jacob Generation. However, I will mostly focus on the Abraham Generation (the Baby Boomers) and Isaac (Generation X), walking together.

JACOB GENERATION: THE MILLENNIALS

According to the insightful, yet sobering, report released by George Barna in October 2021 titled "Millennials in America," the Millennials are often called a "lost generation." Instead of "lost," I believe they are a searching and seeking generation. They are seeking purpose and significance, desperate for identity.

Jacob, in search of his own significance, purpose, and identity in life, deceived his father Isaac and manipulated his older brother Esau to appropriate his birthright. Years later, Jacob wrestled with a man until daybreak (Gen. 32:24). Once he realized the man he was wrestling with was God, he held on until God blessed him. The blessing was the name change from Jacob, which meant "deceiver" or "usurper," to Israel, which means "God prevails" or "triumphant with God."

The Bible calls God "the God of Jacob" a number of times. Then Psalm 53:6 states,

> "Oh, that the salvation of Israel would come out of Zion! When God restores His captive people, let Jacob rejoice, let Israel be glad." (NASB)

What a powerful picture of how God redeems an individual and turns him into a great nation. His plan is redemption for both individuals and nations.

The God of Jacob—He is the Redeemer God. The same God who redeemed Jacob and then turned him into a great nation is also the God who redeems the Millennials. Like Jacob, today's Jacob generation will encounter God, and God will prevail because of the covenant He made with Abraham and Isaac. The Millennials will see the face of God and be preserved (Gen. 32:30).

While there is a great amount of focus on this generation, two previous generations lay the foundation for Jacob, the generation that seeks His face (Psalm 24): Abraham and Isaac.

ABRAHAM AND ISAAC: WALKING TOGETHER

Abraham, the father of faith, holds a key place in the unfolding narrative of the Bible and the history of Israel that continues to impact us today. Through Abraham, God narrows his plan for the world to a specific family. God's plan is to establish His Kingdom on earth through family, from generation to generation. This plan led to blessing for all humanity, including us (Genesis 12:1–3). This promise is reiterated in Genesis 15 and 17. God fulfilled His promise, and Abraham and Sarah bore a son named Isaac well past their child-bearing age. God is often referred to as "the God of Abraham."

Then, in Genesis 22, we find Isaac helping his father Abraham carry the materials needed to make the sacrifice God asked of Abraham. Isaac noticed that Abraham did not bring the lamb to sacrifice but believed his father when he said, "God will provide the sacrifice" (v. 8). Subsequently, Isaac even allowed his father to tie him up, binding his hands and feet together, and then Isaac surely watched his father lift up the knife to sacrifice him—his own son. There is no mention of Isaac resisting, wrestling, fighting, or pushing back. This took great faith from Isaac. Isaac's faith converged with Abraham's faith. God had asked Abraham to sacrifice Isaac on an altar like a goat or sheep, and Abraham agreed. Ultimately, heavenly messengers interfered, delivered Isaac, and recognized Abraham's faith. (See Genesis 22:1-14 for the complete story.)

Two verses I would like to highlight from this passage are the following:

Genesis 22:6: "Abraham took the wood of the burnt offering and laid it on Isaac his son, and he took in his hand the fire and the knife. *So the two of them walked on together*" (italics mine).

Genesis 22:9: "'Abraham said, 'God will provide for Himself the lamb for the burnt offering, my son.' *So the two of them walked on together*'" (italics mine).

Notice the repeated statement: *"So the two of them walked on together."* This is what the generations are called to do—walk together. This is God's heart and intention between the generations.

This is a perfect picture of how the father loves the son, and the son loves the father—how one generation is to love the next and the next, the previous. This is the heart of Malachi 4:5-6:

> Behold, I am going to send you Elijah the prophet before the coming of the great and terrible day of the LORD. He will restore the hearts of the fathers to *their* children and the hearts of the children to their fathers, so that I will not come and smite the land with a curse. (NASB95)

THE ABRAHAM GENERATION – THE BABY BOOMERS

What if the Abraham Generation—the Baby Boomers—are the ones who are to create resources and wealth with God to build? I am not saying that other generations are not given vision and resources. In fact, I feel the Lord has given me, a generation X'er, a God-sized vision and mission. However, we must learn the ways of God and live a life modeling the ways of God, the John 17 mandate of unity and oneness.

Abraham included Isaac, seeing his potential, noticing his strengths, gifts, and even calling. He allowed Isaac to partner with him to fulfill his obedience to God. Abraham was the one who received the promise and created the resources and wealth to build, and Isaac was the one who helped his father.

5 Key Lessons from the Life of Abraham

- Abraham set a spiritual precedence and modeled a life of worship for Isaac. He lived out Psalm 145:4, "One generation shall praise Your works to another, and shall declare Your mighty acts."

- Abraham had the resources to build and fulfill the mandate God gave to him. Abraham did not take from Isaac to fulfill his own vision. In fact, he allowed Isaac to handle the resources and help him build.

- Abraham journeyed with Isaac. Many leaders today have become travel agents, only telling people where to go, rather than travel guides who show people where to go.

- Abraham lived a life of faith, both showing his humanity and believing the goodness of God.

- Abraham leaned into the strength of Isaac's youth while providing wisdom.

7 Characteristics of True Spiritual Fathers and Mothers

- They build resources for their sons and daughters rather than demanding resources from them.

- They take time to guide and disciple, not just point and direct.

- They tell their sons and daughters how great they are, instead of talking about how great *they* (the spiritual father or mother) are.

- They want their sons and daughters to truly exceed and surpass them in every way.

- They are not threatened by their sons and daughters; they promote them.

- They serve them to fulfill their calling, not to "use" them for their own gain.

- They are authentic, vulnerable, and transparent.

THE ISAAC GENERATION: GENERATION X

Isaac was also one of the great patriarchs, the father of Jacob and son of Abraham. We know Jacob as the one who wrestled with God and prevailed—it's a story to remember. Abraham is known as the Father of Nations with whom God first established His covenant. It's a promise to remember. Isaac, on the other hand, can be easily bypassed and overlooked. After all, he is the one who was to be sacrificed.

> By faith Abraham, when he was tested, offered up Isaac, and he who had received the promises was offering up his only begotten *son; it was he* to whom it was said, "IN ISAAC YOUR DESCENDANTS SHALL BE CALLED." He considered that God is able to raise *people* even from the dead, from which he also received him back as a type. (Hebrews 11:17–19 NASB95)

Likewise, Generation X can be easily bypassed and overlooked as they find themselves between two great dominant generations. Many Generation X'ers say they feel like we are the forgotten generation. I don't state this as a disparaging remark; I am just sharing conversations I have had with my fellow Gen X'ers.

Yet Isaac was the one who trusted and obeyed Abraham. He was faithful to his father. He was also father to his own two sons. He was the bridge between Abraham and Jacob. Likewise, Generation X is called to be a bridge between the Millennials and the Boomers. As the bridge, it's paramount for the generations to walk together for the benefit of the following generations.

The modern-day Isaac Generation—Generation X—running with the modern-day Abraham Generation—the Baby Boomers—is key to seeing this Jacob Generation come back to God and fulfill their divine destiny.

The modern-day Isaac Generation—Generation X—running with the modern-day Abraham Generation—the Baby Boomers—is key to seeing this Jacob Generation come back to God and fulfill their divine destiny.

5 Key Lessons from the Life of Isaac:

- Isaac served Abraham even when he didn't fully understand the situation.

- Isaac saw the flaws and humanity of Abraham yet did not disengage and exit the relationship.

- Isaac served Abraham and trusted him even though there was no sign of God providing the sacrifice.

- Isaac leaned into the wisdom of his father.

- Isaac was essential to Abraham fulfilling his calling and mandate of full obedience.

7 Characteristics of True Sons and Daughters:

- They are not opportunists and cannot be bought with a price; they are faithful.

- They carry the heart of their spiritual father and (or) mother by living out the values instilled within them.

- They give their time, talent, and treasure to serve their spiritual father and (or) mother, while building what God has called them to build.

- They are not intimidated by their spiritual father and mother and receive counsel, drawing on their wisdom.

- They protect their spiritual parents from any attacks and criticisms.

- They promote their spiritual parents and invite them to speak into their world.

- They are authentic, vulnerable, and transparent.

THE RISE OF THE SONS OF GOD

"'Jesus said to him, "Have I been so long with you, and yet you have not come to know Me, Philip? He who has seen Me has seen the Father; how can you say, 'Show us the Father'?"'" (John 14:8)

Nowhere in Jesus' statement did He say He was trying to be the Father. Jesus was the Son and remained the Son. When we see the Son, we see the Father. Jesus carried the Father's heart and authority, and was about Father's business. From that position, Jesus, the Son, revealed the Father. The Son of God caused people to experience the Father's love in tangible ways and led people to Him. Now we, who have become sons of God through the Son of God, are to lead people to the Father.

When God highlights a new revelation or movement, we see people's humanity come into play when they try to posture, position, and perhaps self-appoint themselves to these newfound "titles." For example, when God was highlighting the prophets, everyone wanted to be a prophet. When God was highlighting apostles, everyone wanted to be an apostle. Likewise, in a season in which "spiritual fathers" and "spiritual mothers" are being recognized, we see the tendency of human behavior to lean in for significance. After all, we are all created with and for significance.

I have had so many young leaders in their 20s and early 30s introduce me to their "spiritual sons and daughters," thus declaring themselves to be spiritual fathers or mothers. I remember one instance in which a 26-year-old leader introduced me to one of his "spiritual sons" who was close to 60 years old. I found that quite humorous.

I am in no way saying that age is the primary foundation for such a place in someone's life, but maturity is key. May our goal in life be to mature as sons rather than remaining immature leaders.

The truth is, it's difficult to be a good father or mother unless you first learn to be a good son or daughter. Romans 8:19 (NASB95) states, "For the anxious longing of the creation waits eagerly for the revealing of the sons of Go." The very reason apostles and prophets are given as gifts from Christ is to raise up sons and daughters—Kingdom family! I believe the reason we recognize certain persons as spiritual fathers or spiritual mothers is because they are walking as mature sons who carry the heart of Father, thus revealing Him.

5 Lessons I Learned from My Spiritual Father

One person I have had the honor to walk with is my own spiritual father, Ché Ahn. I have now known him for 24 years. I met him through a beautiful woman named Jessica, who is now my wife. I recall sitting in his office meeting him one-on-one for the first time after moving down to Pasadena from the Bay Area (Northern California) in 1998. He asked some life questions, "What do you feel called to?" "What are some of your dreams and passions?"

Lesson 1: True spiritual fathers and mothers care for the hearts of their sons and daughters; therefore, true sons and daughters carry the heart of their spiritual fathers and mothers.

During that conversation, he made a statement that changed my life. He said, "I've never met before a young man who I felt carries a similar calling and anointing as me." This was such an affirmation to me. Every human needs affirmation. Prior to moving to Pasadena, I was told by several pastors that I was not smart enough nor anointed for the ministry; that I was not a good communicator or preacher. It was from that place that Papa Ché affirmed me greatly. This is what happens when a younger generation connects with the father's heart of the previous generation. An affirmation is released that secures us in love.

Lesson 2: True spiritual fathers and mothers see, affirm, and call out the callings and gifts that lie within their spiritual sons and daughters.

In 2009, I was part of the School of Apostles, and each of us had the opportunity to go on an international trip with Papa Ché. I was scheduled to go to Korea, where he was to teach at the Wagner Leadership Institute. A few days before we about to fly out, he communicated that he was not able to go due to a family matter. He told me I was to speak at all of his sessions, along with another person who was set to teach with him.

He, along with Mama Sue Ahn, have always shared about the importance of family— how family is first, next to God. They aren't ones who only talk about it; they live out their convictions and values day in and day out. Of course, they are not perfect, but the fact that he would cancel a major international trip with 300-400 pastors attending this training for the sake of his family made a tremendous impact on me. It is in this relationship that I learned about healthy family. I was challenged to love my wife as the most precious gift given to me from the Lord. I learned being a father to my kids is greater than being a minister to thousands. I learned that we don't sacrifice family for ministry, but because of who we are, as a family we sacrifice together.

Lesson 3: True spiritual fathers and mothers leave a legacy to their sons and daughters—convictions and values of the heart. Therefore, true sons and daughters honor those who have gone before them.

In 2013, I received a call from Papa Ché . He asked me, "What are you doing next week?" I thought he was going to ask me to lunch. I told him, "Well, I could move some of my schedule around if you need me." He said, "Can you go to Taiwan for seven days?" I was surprised. He explained that the main speaker for this national conference had broken his leg and they needed to find another speaker who could teach and move in signs and wonders. He told me he had prayed, and the Holy Spirit led him to call me. This turned out to be a great door that was opened to me.

Lesson 4: True spiritual fathers and mothers open doors to their sons and daughters to fulfill their calling. Therefore, the younger generation must learn to walk with the previous generation.

Incredible miracles, healings, signs, and wonders broke out all week. The fire of God fell for seven days and leaders from other nations began to fly in to receive an impartation. It was that open door through which all of Asia opened up to me, even to this day.

After the trip was over, I called Papa Ché and told him all that had happened. He said the reports had already come in and that he had heard about all that the Holy Spirit had done. He continued to affirm my apostolic call and celebrated me and all that God did. There was no sense of threat or feeling of competition.

> **Lesson 5:** Spiritual fathers and mothers are secure in who they are and celebrate their spiritual sons and daughters. Therefore, true sons and daughters honor and give back to their spiritual fathers and mothers.

CONCLUSION

Before we run together, we must learn to walk together. Before we walk together, we must learn to sit together. May the generations sit, hear, see, and understand one another and cheer each other on. Let's fight and make effort to work together, build together, and serve one another to set up the following generation for success. Hey Abraham! Hey Isaac! There's a Jacob to save! Let's go!

———— ⬥⬥⬥ ————

Chapter Ten

DOUBLE PORTION

Jamie Galloway

Founder
Jamie Galloway Ministries,
Nashville, Tennessee

I will open my mouth in a parable;
I will utter dark sayings of old,
Which we have heard and known,
And our fathers have told us.
We will not hide them from their children,
Telling to the generation to come the praises of the LORD,
And His strength and His wonderful works that He has done.

Psalms 78:2-4

When I was a young boy, my father would take me to work with him. He worked in downtown St. Louis, Missouri, right behind the Soulard Farmers Market. He would give me a couple of dollars and send me, along with my brothers, over to the market to get a bite to eat. The market felt like a magical place to my little kid brain, with people hard at work trying to sell fruits, vegetables, pastries, and all sorts of goodies. It was a lively place. with people all over the place searching for the ingredients for their next food project.

I would then return with my brothers back to my dad's office. About that time, Dad would be in the middle of managing a rush of customers. He would be running back and forth helping his team get everything out to everyone coming through that door. I learned quite a bit just sitting there for hours watching my father lead and manage his team.

It had always been a dream of mine to work with my father. Unfortunately, many do not feel the same way about working with family. They say business and family do not mix. They consider it best to hang with them, but not work with them. If that is you, I want to speak into your destiny and get you back on track with generational blessings. The prophesied spirit of Elijah is here:

> Behold, I will send you Elijah the prophet
> Before the coming of the great and dreadful day of the LORD.
> And he will turn
> The hearts of the fathers to the children,
> And the hearts of the children to their fathers,
> Lest I come and strike the earth with a curse. (Malachi 4:5-6)

Fast forward many years, and I found myself traveling with one of God's Generals, Dr. Randy Clark. I was traveling all over the world with Randy and his team, meeting after meeting, night after night. Just as I'd watched my dad at work, I watched Dr. Clark preach, teach, heal the sick, prophesy, and patiently minister to whoever needed prayer. I would study Dr. Clark's ministry flow and constantly be amazed at the power of God at work through this humble man.

My time with Dr. Clark felt like I was constantly being thrown into the fire to watch God do a supernatural work. There were times when it was just minutes before Randy was about to be invited up on the platform to speak, and he would look over at me with a grin on his face. Nervously, I would approach him and ask what he needed. With only minutes to go before he had to get up there, Dr. Clark would look at me and say with a smile, "How are you doing?" "Fine,"= I would say. "What's up?" "Good," he would say, "because you are preaching tonight." I would kind of laugh nervously as he informed me, "You are on in five minutes."

Dr. Clark's ministry style always kept me on my toes. Working with him was like working with my dad. When it was time to play, it was time to play, but when it was time to work, it was time to work. "You got any words of knowledge?" Dr. Clark would ask. "Yes, I believe so," I would say. "Good, get up there and give them first, and then pray for the sick. After that, go ahead and preach."

Dr. Clark is a firm believer in the Holy Spirit's gift of the "word of knowledge" (1 Cor. 12: 8). Words of knowledge are things God shares with one person about someone else. Then the person who receives the word releases it, as if to inform them that God knows their situation, pain, or illness. Dr. Clark would say, "A word of knowledge is like Jesus walking up to you and saying, "I know your pain, and I want to heal it. If Jesus did that, would you believe? Receive a word of knowledge in the same way."

It was at this time that I realized I had been given a prophetic gift. When I got up in front of everyone to give the words of knowledge I had received from the Holy Spirit, I would end up prophesying to the person for whom I had received the word of knowledge. I would pray for their sickness if needed, but many times the prophetic gift would flow to greatly encourage and strengthen their faith. This was not Dr. Clark's ministry style, but as I honored him and imitated what I saw in my spiritual father, it was as if I had stepped into a double portion.

SMALL BEGINNINGS

"Do not despise these small beginnings, for the Lord rejoices to see the work begin, to see the plumb line in Zerubbabel's hand." (Zechariah 4:10 NLT).

One of the questions I get asked is, "How did you start off in ministry?" Immediately after turning my life over to Jesus, all I wanted to do was share with others the good news of Christ's gospel. I had been set free from so much, and I felt life like I had never felt before. All I wanted to do was share with others. I began volunteering to work for a local evangelist.

Every week, he would need 500-1,000 copies of flyers to give to folks he was ministering to on the streets of St. Louis. I volunteered to work the copy machine at church and make the flyers he needed. I remembered working with my dad's copy machine at his office when I was a kid. This was not something that sat on a desk; it was big, and every time the ink ran out, you had to refill it with these large tubes. With that experience behind me, I knew I could now help this evangelist with his flyers. Every week, I showed up on a Wednesday. Every week, 500-1000 copies of flyers were printed, double sided. I had to manually turn the papers to get the print on the other side. This process would take up a nice portion of the day, but then we got to give the finished product away every week.

One day, my pastor, Randy Clark, asked if he could speak with me. So, at church on Sunday, I stayed over to see what he needed. Randy asked, "Jamie, I am noticing you are using the copy machine quite a bit. Our ledger has your signature on the print log showing you print on a large amount of paper each week. What's going on?" I could tell that Randy was trying to figure out why I was using up the church' resources each week to make all these copies. Hoping I was not in trouble, I said, "Well, yes, that is me. I have been printing up directions to the church to give to people on the streets of St. Louis. There is some information about Jesus on there and directions to the church in case they want to join us for Sundays." Pastor Randy looked surprised. He then asked, "Who is mentoring you?" A little over a year later, Dr. Clark invited me to travel with him and begin a time of mentorship.

DOUBLE PORTION

And so it was, when they had crossed over, that Elijah said to Elisha, "Ask! What may I do for you, before I am taken away from you?"
Elisha said, "Please let a double portion of your spirit be upon me." (2 Kings 2:9)

I want to encourage you, God wants to give you generational blessing. He wants to cause the mantle of one generation to be multiplied in the next generation. This is the double portion and it is realized as one generation walks with another.

I want to encourage you, God wants to give you generational blessing. He wants to cause the mantle of one generation to be multiplied in the next generation. This is the double portion, and it is realized as one generation walks with another.

As simple as it is, it is actually a lot harder than it sounds. When Elisha asks Elijah to give him a double portion of the anointing upon his life, Elijah's response is, "*You have asked a hard thing*" (2 Kings 2:10). Multigenerational blessings require the supernatural grace of God to accomplish them. Whether you are a father or mother, or a son or daughter, if you are on the giving end or the receiving end, imparting a generational inheritance is going to require an extra layer of God's supernatural grace.

Three times, Elijah tried to convince Elisha to move on from him into his own ministry. Elijah was about to be taken by the Lord in a whirlwind to Heaven, but before he went, he stopped at three cities to check on the up-and-coming prophets. Each time, Elijah tried to convince Elisha to stay with the emerging prophets (2 Kings 2:2, 2:4, 2:6). Perhaps he was giving Elisha a purpose, a ministry—seems like a good setup. Elisha would have been treated like royalty in that place. I can imagine the young prophets talking to Elisha: "Whoa man, you traveled with Elijah! What was that like!?" Elisha could have found his place, telling Elijah stories to the emerging prophetic community. But Elisha had something else in his heart. He wanted a double portion.

When Elijah was taken by God into the whirlwind, something transpired between Elijah and Elisha. Elijah's prophetic requirement of Elisha is, "*Nevertheless, if you see me when I am taken from you, it shall be so for you; but if not, it shall not be so*" (2 Kings 2:10). Elisha must see Elijah, but his goal is not just to keep his eyes on Elijah.

Elisha must see *into* Elijah. He will have to peer past the veil of the physical world and see Elijah in the spirit. He has to see beyond the familiar and into the realm of sacred space. He needs to see Elijah in the whirlwind of God's supernatural glory.

> And Elisha saw it, and he cried out, "My father, my father, the chariot of Israel and its horsemen!" So he saw him no more. And he took hold of his own clothes and tore them into two pieces. He also took up the mantle of Elijah that had fallen from him, and went back and stood by the bank of the Jordan. Then he took the mantle of Elijah that had fallen from him, and struck the water, and said, "Where is the LORD God of Elijah?" And when he also had struck the water, it was divided this way and that; and Elisha crossed over. (2 Kings 2:12-14)

God wants to give you eyes to see the Elijahs and Elishas who have been assigned to your life. He wants to remove the veil and let you see what He sees about those God has given you.

Partnership

> For though you might have ten thousand instructors in Christ, yet you do not have many fathers; for in Christ Jesus I have begotten you through the gospel. Therefore I urge you, imitate me. For this reason I have sent Timothy to you, who is my beloved and faithful son in the Lord, who will remind you of my ways in Christ, as I teach everywhere in every church. (1 Corinthians 4:15-17)

The apostle Paul was brilliant at creating partnerships. The Corinthian church needed someone to come and invest spiritual life into their community. Paul could have easily taken on the task himself; after all, he had planted the church at Corinth. However, Paul instructs them to receive from the ministry of Timothy as though it were him. Paul is looking to multiply his influence with the Corinthian believers and speaks to them as a father, "Therefore I urge you, imitate me. For this reason I have sent Timothy to you" (1 Corinthians 4:16-17). Paul's continued partnership with the Corinthians is multiplied through the effect of his spiritual sons and daughters.

Something special is happening in this generation. Like the apostle Paul, many fathers and mothers in the faith are hearing the call to partner with the next generation. And, like Timothy, many sons and daughters are being positioned into an alignment in their spirit to partner with the generations.

ALIGNMENT

"The lines have fallen to me in pleasant places; Yes, I have a good inheritance." (Psalms 16:6)

You may have heard it said, "alignment for the assignment." However, alignment is very often the assignment. Get aligned to the "who" God has given to you.

Have you ever had a car with the steering out of alignment? I have. My off road truck can handle quite a bit, but some time ago it startled wobbling and shuddering. I noticed it would seem to turn even though I was driving straight. I could not figure out what was going on, but something told me it was the alignment. I went in, and sure enough, the auto shop confirmed it was an issue with the alignment. After fixing it up, they informed me I would need four new tires because two of them had worn unevenly, and the tread was wearing off of them.

If you aren't moving forward at the speed you have believed for, it is time to get re-aligned to the assignment and the generations God has called you to. God wants to give you a double portion! You're going to need eyes to see the "lines" God has given you in "pleasant places" (Psalm 16:6). God is getting ready to set you up for divine partnership.

When Generations Run Together
is available for purchase at Amazon.com

Elizabeth Tiam-Fook can be contacted at:
generationsbook222@gmail.com

International Young Prophets
P.O. Box 1351
Maricopa, Arizona 85139
www.internationalyoungprophets.com

Made in the USA
Las Vegas, NV
18 April 2022

47675376R00085